the Game Changer

the
Game
Changer

A Business Parable about
Transformational Business Design

Chicke Fitzgerald

NEW YORK

NASHVILLE • MELBOURNE • VANCOUVER

the Game Changer
A Business Parable about Transformational Business Design

Published in New York, New York, by Morgan James Publishing. Morgan James is a trademark of Morgan James, LLC. www.MorganJamesPublishing.com

The Morgan James Speakers Group can bring authors to your live event. For more information or to book an event visit The Morgan James Speakers Group at www.TheMorganJamesSpeakersGroup.com.

ISBN 978-1-68350-496-2 paperback
ISBN 978-1-68350-497-9 eBook
Library of Congress Control Number: 2017903501

Cover Design by:
Rachel Lopez
www.r2cdesign.com

Interior Design by:
Bonnie Bushman
The Whole Caboodle Graphic Design

In an effort to support local communities, raise awareness and funds, Morgan James Publishing donates a percentage of all book sales for the life of each book to Habitat for Humanity Peninsula and Greater Williamsburg.

Get involved today! Visit
www.MorganJamesBuilds.com

Inspired by the dreamers, the rebels and the crazy ones who refuse to settle for business as usual and truly believe you can change the world.

Dedicated to my family and friends and the "village" that love me unconditionally as I am, continue to provide a circle of strength and who never, ever give up on me—endless gratitude.

Table of Contents

Foreword

If you have ever tried to build a business, joined an early stage company, or invested in a business, you know that the leadership team and employees face immense challenges at every stage of the company's development. If the company is growing, it is still hard, but you are one of the lucky ones. If the company is failing, it's not only harder, it is much less rewarding and a lot more stressful. The fact is that nearly 9 out of 10 startups in the U.S. fail. And the average "overnight success" takes eight years.

In *the Game Changer,* Chicke Fitzgerald applies what she has learned from her personal and professional successes and failures to craft a story about transformational business design. The result of that design is a culture of joy, enjoyed by the staff, customers, and investors alike.

Chicke's experience creating and leading startups, coupled with her track record as an innovation leader with American Airlines Sabre, Worldspan and SITA, give her a very broad perspective on the challenges companies and teams face at all stages of the game. She adeptly brings those experiences and perspectives to the story of Avi and his team as they struggle to grow their software company, even after taking in outside investment.

The allegorical writing style in *the Game Changer* makes it a personal journey as well as a business book.

As readers, we can all identify with the characters and the dynamics across the team. You will have plenty of *Oh yeah, I've been there*, moments as you read this book. The characters' backstories frame their points of view and outline their strengths and weaknesses and their roles in the current business. Because each character helps personalize the learning and make the lessons relevant, any business professional will relate to the story and enjoy the read.

Reading this book, you will be exposed to snippets of other great business and marketing books and get the themes and highlights from a host of bestselling business and leadership authors. This interweaving of Chicke's real-life interviews with top authors and the key points from other authors' books is a unique approach to delivering her message. It is also a testament to her personal leadership style—learning from other leaders and acknowledging those game-changers' impact in her personal and professional life.

The author's goal was to make *the Game Changer* an easy, yet impactful, read and it is. You will learn something valuable in each chapter and get tips that you will be able to apply in your business that same day. Use *the Game Changer* to identify the challenges in your business and your team and set the course to your next level of success. After all, that is Chicke's goal as a game changer— **to accelerate your success and to give you the courage to write your own aspirational story**.

Bob Burg

Coauthor, *The Go-Giver*

Prologue

Living the Dream

This is surreal. I am on the stage and as I step into position, I realize that I have been dreaming about this for more than ten years. Even though I am comfortable with public speaking, I find that I simply have to stop and take a breath. A very deep breath.

What am I experiencing? A strange mix of fear and joy.

Out there, in front of me, are over one thousand people—sitting, waiting for me to open my mouth, dazzle them with my story and end with something truly profound. No pressure there.

Thank God the lights make their faces all but invisible to me. But I know they're there. I'm grateful that in the front row are my family, my team and those that make up the board of directors of my life. They give me strength to go beyond my comfort zone.

The music playing the background is David Bowie's *Changes*. The mood in the room is high. The excitement is palpable, a steady drumbeat of thrill and anticipation. Or perhaps it is just the pounding of my own heart. The pressure is on.

Behind me is an enormous screen with an image of a chess board, populated with dominos. Superimposed over it is the title of my talk, "My Life as a Game Changer." I laugh to myself. *Do you supposed they will realize the obviousness of the dominos not being the normal chess pieces? I hope that the audience will get it.*

Beside me are three, enormous red letters, one flowing into the next that have to be five feet tall each.

I pause. In the few seconds before I utter the first words that open my talk, I see years and months leading up to this moment flashing before my eyes. After I published my book and my company went public, the press had described me as overnight success, but it had in fact taken more than a decade to get from where I started to this stage.

For years, I had faithfully articulated the words, "I am the CEO of a well-funded technology company in Tampa, Florida," both in my head and out loud. Sometimes I said it many times in a single day. There were days when it felt real. There were many more when it felt like nonsense.

I kept saying it. And now, here I am.

I resist the urge to pinch myself. I am living the dream. I am giving a TED talk.

■ ■ Here | Now ■ ■

I must admit that in the beginning, I was simply wishing success into existence.

I had served the travel industry faithfully for nearly four decades. The first eighteen years, I was an executive with the technology companies that had changed the way people planned travel. The last twenty had been as entrepreneur and strategic consultant to many companies using that same underlying technology to power new generations of trip planning systems.

Then, ten years ago, I had an idea to take trip planning beyond where even the industry giants that I had worked, both for and with, had taken it.

Through sheer grit and determination, I built it from an idea into a product, pivoting multiple times as I juggled my day job as a consultant and my dreams of turning an industry on its head with my game changing product.

Several years ago, I paused to take stock of where I was, and where I was going. I wanted to make sure that I was not going to end up as one of those entrepreneurs that worked eighty hours a week, just to avoid working forty hours a week for someone else.

I had to admit that at the time, my vision of a "well-funded company" was no more than a product. And it certainly was not well funded. The dream felt elusive, but I continued to press on.

The significance of wanting that company to be based in Tampa was two-fold. First, Tampa was not exactly known as a major hub for tech investment, and I didn't want to take in outside investors that might force me to arbitrarily move the headquarters elsewhere. Perhaps more importantly, I had been working on a virtual basis for more than twenty years and I had enough of managing by conference call. I had worked out of my home for years, and I was ready to get back in an office environment—to be a real company, with an actual, physical team.

While the rest of the world was wanting to get out of their offices and have the freedom to work from home, here I was, wanting exactly the opposite. Community, momentum, brainstorming and the energy that came with working with a physical team were my heart's desires.

Over the last ten years there were small wins that kept me going, but there were also missteps and even a spectacular failure on the path to my success. So many that had preceded me told me that failure was not only a rite of passage, it was actually a necessary part of the entrepreneurial journey.

I had mastered "failing fast." I was ready to succeed and I was ready to experience the pure joy of knowing that I had reached that important milestone, the top of my very own mountain.

I did eventually take in investment. A small amount at first to keep the dream alive and later more to fuel the vision. Without it, I might still be at the base of the mountain, still planning how to reach the heights, simply imagining the joy of the summit experience.

Based on the advice of many successful entrepreneurs, I waited for the larger capital raise, not only until I had released the minimum viable product and completed the proof of concept with launch clients in our target sectors, but also until the company was cash flow positive, funded out of revenues. I couldn't have done that without my core team, our partners, my board and advisory board members. Oh, and I can't forget my family and dear friends.

Whew. It wasn't easy, but I did it. Or should I say, *we* did it.

Of all the learning along the way, I knew that the most important takeaway was that I can't travel this road alone. The entrepreneurial journey must include others. Many others. And not just my team. There were many unexpected travelers that came alongside me along the way.

I call them my Executive Village, as I truly could not live without them.

I have not given that TED talk yet, but I am certainly looking forward to it. I look forward to telling it, because I know my story is unique.

Just like your story is unique. Perhaps one day you will stand on that stage, ready to tell your own tale.

Mine began as a college dropout, took me to a career with some great travel tech companies and on to being the CEO of my own multi-million-dollar consulting firm. I then became a radio show host and author, and now I am a tech entrepreneur, launching my 2nd tech company.

The steps I have taken, when viewed individually, may seem unremarkable, but when put together, they tell quite the tale.

These elements of my own story and those that make up your own experience are in fact a tapestry. From the back, it may look like a bunch of knots, with no real plan. But when looked at in landscape view from the eyes of the One that wove it, it is transformed into a work of art. You will find that the story is quite amazing.

What I have learned through the collection of my own experience is that playing the same old game leads to the same old results—and that, once you understand how to walk out onto a chessboard and turn it into a game of dominoes, the world is your oyster.

I also learned that a successful company is built not by one or more founders with their vision, grit and determination, nor is it made by the money invested in that company. It is built by a village—some would call it a tribe.

That is the story I will tell on the stage when my day comes. And I look forward to hearing your story and hearing you describe how you created your extraordinary success by gathering your own amazing team, creating your own village and changing the game in your own industry.

I learned how to become a game changer.

In the little story that follows, I want to show you how you can become one, too.

It all began, one day a few years ago, when a small struggling tech firm, trying to change the world with its innovative trip planning tools, takes in private equity. Together they embark on a journey that begins with an offsite strategy session that has gone terribly wrong...

Chapter 1

Capturing the Moment

■ ■ Tampa | May 2016 | Catherine, VP Product Innovation ■ ■

Catherine's day had started at six that morning at the gym with her personal trainer. That was one of the benefits of company offices in the building next to the Grand Hyatt on Tampa Bay—being able to use the hotel gym facilities. That and getting a great cup of coffee at the café when she was finished with her workout.

Today she was especially grateful to avoid the gym in her neighborhood. The parking lot had been packed this morning as she drove by. *You'd would think it was January*, she thought, *with everyone still trying to keep their New Year's resolutions*—but the date on her iPhone's screen clearly read May 27.

It was easy to forget the time of year here in Tampa. This morning the temperature was a balmy 75 degrees, with very low humidity, but when she asked Siri for the forecast, "she" said it was going to reach 95 today. Yes, summertime in Tampa had definitely arrived. Catherine enjoyed the walk from the car to the office where she would meet her trainer.

She was training to climb Mt. Kilimanjaro, the tallest, free-standing peak in the world. It was one of her bucket list items. Her husband, Andy, thought she was crazy, but he had learned long ago to let her follow her dreams. Everyone was happier that way.

Two days a week they worked out with weights in the gym to build both upper and lower body strength, which she would need for the climb. Because Tampa was a very flat place, the other three days, her trainer had her running up and down the stairs, spanning the fourteen stories of the office building. And not just run, but run wearing a fifty-pound backpack. She could still feel the burning in her lungs as she reached the thirteenth floor, not sure that she'd make it another flight. But she did it. Just barely.

The training schedule was brutal, and she loved it. She was as fit as she had ever been, and although the stairs had kicked her butt this morning, she felt strong and energized after her session. And strangely confident. She could do this.

Tonight, however, was a different story. Catherine was tired. It was that deep feeling that went much further than anything physical. Despite her burst of confidence this morning, that little voice was back, telling her, *You're not enough.* Some days it was that she wasn't a good enough wife, or educated enough. Now, it was the mom version.

After yet another day of back-to-back offsite meetings, Catherine finally got back to her office at 6:30 p.m., realizing that she had missed her daughter's soccer game. Again. She was especially distraught because this was the district championship game.

Earlier that day, when she realized her meeting was running long and she might not get there on time, she had left Andy a voicemail asking him to pick up their son from tennis practice at four. She hated having to ask him to cut his day short, but there was just no other way around it. And anyway, the tennis courts were right near his office in Feather Sound, so it was on his way to the soccer field at Tampa University, where the championships were playing.

She hoped they had made it to the game in time so that Veronica wouldn't be the only player without a parent there to cheer her on.

With Andy's travel schedule, Catherine sometimes experienced what a single parent must feel, trying to excel at work, while keeping on top of the kids' grades and sports. Thank God they had someone to clean the house and do laundry. Catherine didn't think that she could manage that on top of everything else.

Thankfully, after nineteen years of marriage, Andy knew her limits. They had actually been together a total of twenty-five years, since the end of her sophomore year of high school at Pulaski High in Milwaukee. Their only time apart had been the years that they went away to college—she to Northwestern in nearby Chicago, and Andy to Florida State in Tallahassee.

Can that have been almost twenty years ago?

Catherine had graduated from high school a full year early at seventeen. That is how old Veronica was now.

Andy was a year older, so they graduated at the same time—May, 1993. Their parents had urged them to go to different schools before making any commitments to one another.

Tallahassee had one of the highest placement rates in the country for sales professionals. Andy loved sales. Even in high school he had always been the top sales person on every fundraiser. In his decision-making process, it didn't hurt that FSU had a great football team. Although he didn't play football, Andy was a fanatical fan. He was looking forward to being a Seminole, even though it meant being so far away from Catherine.

Catherine was very happy with Andy's choice of school, since it was such a perfect match for his goals. Plus, when she was on break from her marketing and business studies, she would visit Florida, escaping the mind-numbing snow and bitter winters in Evanston, Illinois.

They had promised their parents they would wait until they graduated from college to get married. True to that promise, they were married on July 23, 1997. It was a doubly special day for her, as it was her parent's anniversary as well.

Veronica was Catherine's oldest child. She and Andy had only been married just over a month when she found out that she was pregnant. She had heard jokes about honeymoon babies, but she never thought that it would be a part of her story! Of course, she also had never imagined marrying her high school sweetheart, but she had.

Andy had taken a semester off after graduation, but had already been accepted into the prestigious graduate program at FSU for sales leadership. Their program was designed to allow college graduates to do a one semester sales internship before starting the program in January. The architects of the program felt that it would be much more successful if their students had a taste of the real world when they entered in January. She remembered back to the Sunday that Andy had come home from a meeting with a colleague to tell her about his new job.

■ ■ Milwaukee | August 1997| Catherine and Andy ■ ■

"Catherine, you'll never guess what happened! Today after our football game, we went out for a beer with the other team and I was offered an internship with Harley-Davidson in their sales training department. They know that I've been accepted into graduate school and are fine with the timing. It will look really great on my resume!"

Catherine held back tears but managed a smile after she hugged him, perhaps a little longer than he might have expected with a congratulatory hug. On the way to church that morning, they heard on the radio that Princess Diana had died. She hoped that he would attribute her emotions to that, as she had always been fascinated with the royals and Diana's life story.

Now of course, that wasn't it. She had been impacted by the news on the radio, but it was her own news that was the issue. She couldn't possibly ask him to stay home and be Mr. Mom now. She would have to find another time to share her news with him so that she could consider her own future, in light of his news. She made reservations for the following night at their favorite German restaurant, near the Marquette campus. She would tell him then.

When Catherine and Andy walked into the restaurant, the hostess took them straight to their regular table. Andy immediately saw the bottle of champagne on ice and smiled. "Before you get too excited, you might want to look at the label." said Catherine.

Andy sat down and reached for the bottle immediately. The bottle had a unique label on it that was not familiar to him. It was sparkling cider and the label had a picture of a smiling stork and a balloon with the words, "Congratulations Daddy!" In smaller print, under the balloon were the words "Sorry, no alcohol for the new mommy!"

Andy jumped up right away. Catherine hadn't yet sat down, as she was taking off her jacket and putting it on the unoccupied chair with her purse. As she turned to sit down, he hugged her and put a tender hand on her belly. "Babe, I can't believe it! I didn't think that things could get any better, but I was wrong!" They were both oblivious to the people sitting around them until they all started clapping. They both started laughing at the same time.

In the booth to their right was someone taking a video of the whole thing. The videographer popped the video cartridge out and put it on the table as he hugged them both. It was labeled, "The Baby Announcement—August 1997." She mouthed, "Thank you" to the videographer and turned her attention back to Andy.

"Catherine, you thought of absolutely everything!" said Andy. Catherine smiled and said to her husband, "You know Andy, since having a family quickly hadn't been a part of our plans, I want you to know right now that I am going to drop out of graduate school at the end of the first semester so that I can get everything packed and get us settled in Tallahassee. Then perhaps I will do some volunteering until the baby is born in mid-April. That will help me make friends, which you know is tough for me." Andy leaned forward, grasped her hand tenderly and responded, "Catherine, I do know that it is hard for you, but I really don't understand your insecurities. You are nothing short of amazing."

Brushing off the complement, she interrupted Andy with her bigger news, "Andy, I want you to know that I plan to just stay home with the baby, at least for the first two years." Catherine saw that Andy was surprised and even a little choked up, but instinctively she knew that it was because he was very happy. All through high school he had talked about having kids and how great it would be that she would stay at home with them. At the time, she didn't have the courage to tell him that she really wanted to get her MBA and pursue her own career. And now here she was giving up that dream.

The waiter came and took their beverage order and went over the specials. Catherine was famished.

After a few moments, Andy said, "Wow babe, I still can't believe it. April? I'm still taking everything in. I know it will be hard for you putting your graduate degree on hold, but you know my parents both worked when I was little." She remembered him telling stories of his dad traveling so much while managing the ROTC programs at all the University of Wisconsin campuses and his mom never being home when he was sick, as she taught at Marquette.

He interrupted her thoughts. "I just can't see putting our baby in daycare with strangers."

Catherine had barely finished orientation at Kellogg School of Management at Northwestern when she found out that she was pregnant and she knew that Andy would feel this way. Plus, he would never want her commuting every day from Milwaukee to the northern suburb of Chicago. She was reluctant to quit, but she knew that it was the best solution, since they wouldn't have any family around once they moved to Tallahassee.

Catherine sighed. "Andy, I have so many emotions swirling around inside. I am excited about the baby, but also not looking forward to telling my parents that we are leaving Milwaukee. It will kill my mother to find out that I am pregnant with their first grandchild and moving more than a thousand miles away. Now we won't be around for her to enjoy the baby."

Andy responded "Catherine, she can come and visit and you know that your twin brother and your younger sister won't be far behind in getting started with their families, so maybe your mom will be okay with our move after all." Catherine looked dubious. "Well, I can hope anyway!" Andy said with optimism in his voice. That optimism was one of the things that she loved most about him.

■ ■ Milwaukee | January 1998 | Catherine and Avi ■ ■

Catherine met Avi, the founder and CEO of her current company just five months later.

They were still living in Milwaukee. She was nearly six months pregnant. She had been invited to Avi's lecture at Marquette University by a dear friend and gladly took a break from packing. Andy's mom would be there too, as she managed the business school program that brought in visiting speakers from around the world.

She and Andy were moving on January 25 to Tallahassee. It was an odd coincidence, and she pondered the significance because twice during her childhood they had moved on that very same date. It definitely marked the start of another new chapter in her life. New beginnings.

Avi was an imposing figure and when she first met him, Catherine had what can only be described as a visceral reaction to him, knowing instinctively that he would have a significant impact on her life. It wasn't just his six foot two stature and dark, good looks, or the fact that he had the deep, booming voice of a radio announcer. There was just something about him that inspired confidence, even though they had just met.

■ ■ Israel | January 1951- August 1972 | Avi ■ ■

He was born Abraham David. The year was 1951. He had been called Avi since he was a little boy. He spent his early years in a village just on the outskirts of Jerusalem, where his father was an innkeeper and his mother ran an alterations shop.

While they always had whatever they truly needed, money was definitely not plentiful. He remembered being embarrassed on the first day of school at Henrietta Szold Elementary School. He was wearing clothes that his mother had made. The other kids often teased him about that and the fact that they lived in the back of the inn.

His neighbor, Benjamin, who was two years older and had just moved to Jerusalem from the US, always stood up for him. As a result, despite the difference in their ages, they became good friends and Avi loved to hear his stories about life in Philadelphia where he had lived before they came back to Israel.

In 1962, just as Avi was entering his last year of primary school, his dad was hired by Hilton, an American hospitality company. The family moved to Tel Aviv.

Avi was so excited. He still remembered the day he found out about it. He could still hear his mother saying "It is an answer to our prayers. Imagine! A small house on the waterfront promenade near Independence Park!"

The house was near where Hilton was building a new hotel on the cliff overlooking the Mediterranean. This was a new level of prosperity for their family, and that year Avi enjoyed his first store bought school clothes. They had turned a huge corner.

Avi's favorite uncle was the foreman of the construction crew and always found odd jobs for Avi to do on the site. He was there on the day that they broke ground in September of 1962 and became very close friends with many of the construction workers, who grew used to having the lanky pre-teen in his hard hat on the construction site, ready to help wherever he could.

Avi would never forget when he heard the heartbreaking news that his uncle Levi was killed in a construction accident on the seaside building site. Two other workers that he knew well were also killed in the tragic mishap.

When the hotel opened three years later, his father was appointed General Manager. Avi remembered the new navy blue suit and the red tie that his father bought for him to attend the grand opening. And best of all, he got to meet Prime Minister Eshkol. They even shared a table with him at the dinner! It was, without a doubt, the high point of his young life. He would have to write to Benjamin and tell him, as Avi knew he had a dream of one day becoming Prime Minister of Israel.

From his fifteenth birthday onward, Avi worked for his father after school, on weekends, and during all his school holidays; learning the hospitality business literally from the ground up. In his work, he met internationally renowned musicians, movie stars, singers, artists, sports champions, and statesmen, many of them from the US. All his friends were star struck with the celebrities, but for him, it was the politicians that captured his attention.

He saved most of the money that he made working at the hotel as a down payment on his dream of attending university in America. While he loved Israel, he felt something inexplicably drawing him across the Atlantic. He still dreamed of pursuing a career in politics, but as a backup plan, he felt that a degree in technology would be more practical. He could always minor in political science.

■ ■ Boston | August 1972 | Avi ■ ■

Avi had come to the US in August of 1972 to attend MIT after the thirty months of his compulsory military service. True to his plan, he majored in Information Technology, with a minor in Political Science. His good friend and early protector Benjamin, came to MIT the same year, studying Architecture and Management. He was in his Political Science classes, as he shared Avi's fascination with politics. It was good to have a familiar face nearby. It had been a long time since they had seen one another. After moving to the US in 1963, his friend had returned after high school for his compulsory service. But unlike Avi, Benjamin had trained in the special forces, so they didn't serve together. It was good to reunite and he looked forward to catching up.

Avi was fortunate to be introduced by a friend of the family to the head of the IT department, Professor Madnick, who took him under his wing. During Avi's sophomore year, Madnick published an article in the Sloan Management Review titled, *Technical Advances in the Computer Industry and Their Future Impact*. Avi was fascinated and vowed to get his own paper about innovation published someday.

During the summer after his sophomore year, Avi watched the Watergate hearings with great fascination. He had met Richard Nixon briefly at the hotel when he and his wife had been on vacation, just before he started campaigning for President. In retrospect, with the plethora of anti-Semitic remarks from Nixon that were exposed during the hearings, Avi found it odd that they had chosen Tel Aviv for their vacation.

On October 6 of his junior year, Avi woke up to shocking news. Egypt and Syria had attacked Israel.

He called home right away. Everyone was fine. His dad even said that business was good. He reminded Avi of the resilience of the travel industry and its need for technology solutions. Then the phone rang and it was Benjamin, telling him that his Sayeret Matkal special forces unit had been called up and he was returning to Israel to fight. He promised that he would be back as soon as he could. Avi reminded him to be careful, knowing that he was heading into a very dangerous situation.

In the coming days after the start of what would later be known as the Yom Kippur War, Nixon played a pivotal role in protecting Israel and against all odds, he got Congress to approve the infamous Operation Nickel Grass airlift.

Avi heard later that Prime Minister Golda Meir, the strong willed, straight talking leader who had been referred to by former Prime Minister Ben Gurion as the "best man in government," admitted to crying when she heard about the airlift. Avi had met her at the hotel at a dinner celebrating her inauguration just before he left to do his military service. She was a formidable woman, but had been very kind to him.

Nineteen days after it started, the war was over, in large part due to the Nickel Grass airlift operations. His American Government professor told his class that although there was real risk to Nixon politically in pushing for the support, he recognized that the defeat of Israel was unthinkable for US interests. The professor called Nixon's decision to aid Israel "a true profile in courage."

Through his support of Israel in that conflict, Nixon had redeemed himself somewhat in Avi's mind. He tucked away the fact that true leadership meant that *you didn't always get to do what was popular, but you always needed to do what was right.*

The following August, Nixon resigned the Presidency, having been exposed for multiple abuses of power. Upon learning of the resignation, the next day when he watched the morning news, Avi suddenly realized that his desire to pursue a career in politics was gone. He turned off the television and called the school to ask if it was too late to register for the Ethics class that his business professor had told him about.

Benjamin had come back to MIT in 1975 and despite taking time off for the Yom Kippur War, he finished his four-year degree in architecture and an advanced degree at Sloan in just two-and-a-half years. He was working simultaneously on a doctorate in Political Science at Harvard, but wasn't able to finish because his brother Yonatan was killed in Operation Entebbe. Avi hadn't known him, but was sad nevertheless to hear of Benjamin's loss.

After graduating with honors from MIT in 1975, Avi had worked for the early tech leader, and now defunct, Digital Equipment Company. After more than two decades at DEC, which had sponsored his permanent immigration to the US, Compaq acquired the company's assets. While Avi hoped that his job would be safe, many of his colleagues, including his boss, were already actively looking for a job. Avi didn't want to be without a safety net for the first time since coming to the US, so instead of being a victim of his circumstances, he was in the early stages of forming what would be his first company.

■ ■ Milwaukee | 1998 | Catherine ■ ■

Catherine first encountered Avi on January 4, 1998. She remembered it, as it was Andy's birthday.

Avi was lecturing at a local university on breakthrough technology and its ability to transform entire industries. He was still at DEC, and although he could not yet share it publicly, he was now certain that his days at DEC were numbered.

In his talk, Avi shared a story from the late '80s about a product that a division of AMR, American Airlines, in Dallas had introduced to Avi's business applications development group within DEC. The head of the division at American was Max Hopper, one of his heroes. Max was the acknowledged father of airline computer reservations systems.

The application of computers to business processes had intrigued Avi since 1973, when Hilton had developed the first centralized reservation service for hotels. This had dramatically transformed customer service in his dad's hotel in Tel Aviv.

"When I was at MIT, one of the projects that intrigued Professor Madnick was the Sabre case study. He wanted to write a book on the strategic use of information technology and his friend Professor James Cash from Harvard told him that Max Hopper was the first person that defined the marketing leverage that could come from technology. So, Cash went to New York to see him. Hopper had just been recruited as Director of Sabre for American Airlines, but had also worked on the United Airlines reservation system when he was with EDS." There was a long pause and then Avi said, almost reverently, "I have to admit that I idolized Max Hopper."

Avi continued, "He retired in 1995 as Chairman of the Sabre Group, the American Airlines' information technology unit that provided booking technology to travel agencies worldwide. He was cited in the Harvard Business Review as the driving visionary force behind the evolution of airline reservations systems into centralized information and booking systems for the travel industry. He was credited with *defining an era*."

That told her everything she needed to know about why Avi idolized him.

Next Avi shared his story from his group at DEC and their involvement with the Capture team. "It was one of the first business applications developed on the UNIX platform, which was a mainstay of the DEC world. It was a tool that nearly every company in the world could potentially use, no matter their size. You need to pay attention to ideas that have such broad application and that are truly a utility."

Avi had the entire room enthralled as he shared anecdotes about the Capture product team.

"The woman that led Capture told me a story when I first met her. On the day that she first presented the Capture project to Max Hopper, when he asked what operating system it ran on, she sheepishly said UNIX. At that exact moment, Hopper's secretary came in to say that he had a call from Bob Crandall, the CEO of American. When he came back into the room, he forgot about the operating system question and moved on. She sighed a huge sigh of relief, as Hopper was well known as a fan of IBM. The UNIX thing could have been a deal killer.

"Later, after getting not only Hopper's approval, but getting a five-million-dollar commitment from Bob Crandall, the Capture product lead formed a skunkworks group, and got permission to work out of an apartment in Hayward, California. It was across the Bay from what is now called Silicon Valley. The core product had been acquired from a company there, so this provided access to the original tech team and the founders.

"The product would have completely revolutionized how business travelers processed their expense reports. In the late '80s, the PC had not yet penetrated corporate America, and if you can imagine it, filing and approval of expenses were still done manually! The Capture system would aggregate information from various sources online, and it automated the approval process and integrated the resulting payment request directly into a company's accounting systems."

Avi continued, "DEC was excited about not only testing the product internally, but also saw the potential of having our platform used around the world to give individuals within a corporation access to a system that would simplify this process end-to-end. In this PC-driven world, I know that it is hard to imagine a time when that wasn't the norm."

"The concept was way ahead of its time and working on development in the living room of an apartment was completely unorthodox. It was unusual for a major company like AMR to authorize such an adventure, but Hopper knew that you had to plant seeds of innovation and nurture them to facilitate growth.

"When I was young I dreamed of being a statesman, but the more that I learned about Hopper's life, I knew that I wanted to be a tech leader, and not just any leader, but one that left a legacy."

Avi had slowed his speech as he mentioned Hopper's name again, then looked slowly around the room. He continued in a soft tone that made everyone listen even more intently to his deep voice. Catherine remembered this technique from her communications class. He had masterfully captured the moment and in that instant, he owned the audience.

Avi started speaking slowly. "It would still be another few years before PCs were a mainstay in corporations."

When he said that, Catherine remembered that DEC's founder and CEO Ken Olsen had missed the personal computer opportunity, being very vocal that there wasn't a place in the home for a computer. She wondered what Avi thought about that since Apple Computer, IBM and even Radio Shack had beaten DEC to that punch, clearly proving Olsen wrong. She didn't have to wait long for her answer.

Avi's next comment came with a wry smile. "Although I will deny it if anyone asks, it was very frustrating for me that DEC could have been the thought leader in incorporating this tool into our business application suite. Had we been focusing our research and development efforts on personal computing versus the classic enterprise mainframe focus of the company, things would have turned out very differently for my company. Ken Olsen, our founder and fellow

MIT graduate, was both an innovator and an entrepreneur, but on the topic of computing in the home, that particular boat sailed without us."

Avi swiftly went on and talked about entrepreneurialism versus "intrapreneurialism" and what happens when a skunkworks project is formed within a large company to create innovative products and solutions.

One thing Catherine remembered distinctly from this section of his talk was his statement, "These kinds of think tanks are vital to moving forward with new ideas, but so often are not given enough resources and runway to succeed."

Avi had continued the story, and recounted that in late 1987, just when they were ready to roll out the product to the entire DEC sales and service team, he got a call from the woman that was the CEO of the skunkworks project.

She had said to him "Avi, I am so sorry to have to deliver this news. I can hardly believe it myself, but Bob Crandall, the CEO of AMR and American Airlines, just shut the Capture venture down in his quarterly staff meeting today, with absolutely no advanced notice. I knew that you were the first call that I had to make."

Avi shared with the crowd, "I was touched that she had called me first, as I knew that both Sun Mircrosystems and Unisys were also in the beta test group for the product." The crowd laughed at this and Avi smiled. "My momentary pride at being first was quickly overshadowed by the fact that this was a high-profile project for me and truly I was stunned by the news. Moreover, it felt like the death of a dream. Max Hopper had agreed to come to Boston that fall to attend the sales meeting where the product launch would be announced. But with that phone call, I knew that my dream would not be fulfilled."

Even though more than a decade had passed, as Avi related the story of the cancellation of the Capture project, Catherine could still hear raw emotion in his voice.

Avi's next words made a huge impression on her, "Despite the setback, it fueled my commitment to carry on the seed of innovation that project had planted in my soul."

Avi finished his speech by saying that he had lost track of the woman that led that project, but he hoped that she had landed well. "I knew from our call that day that she had to let go over 90 staff, which had to be a heartbreaking experience for her. I can relate to her situation personally, as most of you know DEC has announced publicly today that it is looking for a suitor and cutbacks and tightening up are now the order of the day."

Catherine was impressed with the transparency with which Avi had shared his story and privately hoped she would never have to go through that experience. But she did want to hear more about what Avi had done with the "seed of innovation" planted in his soul that day in 1987 and she wondered whether he had ever met Max Hopper face to face.

Chapter 2

Holding on to Hope

■ ■ Milwaukee | January 1998 | Catherine and Avi ■ ■

After the talk that day in 1998, Andy's mom Clare ushered Catherine to the reception room behind the main auditorium. She knew that Catherine would want to meet Avi, and there were some VIPs that were invited to speak with him privately. Clare whispered to her that it was Avi's birthday. Catherine found it funny that Avi and Andy shared a birthday. She thanked her mother-in-law for info and for the privilege, and gave her a hug, thinking about how much she would miss her when they moved to Tallahassee.

As she waited in line, she realized that this was a pivotal moment for her. A little voice inside of her told her that she was just star struck by this handsome, deep-voiced man, and that she should just turn now while she still had the chance. She had to fight the urge to listen to the all too familiar voice of insecurity.

When she reached the front of the line she said, "My name is Catherine. I just wanted to tell you how much your story impacted me. I think a lot about innovation and am amazed at how so many companies are satisfied with the status quo and incremental change. They would never take the kind of risk that you described to form a skunkworks to do research and development in groundbreaking areas, let alone allow the team to work out of an apartment instead of corporate headquarters." He just smiled and nodded. She paused, and then said, "I am curious as to what has happened with the innovation seed that you talked about from that project you did with the company in Texas?"

Avi smiled that she said all that without taking a breath and then surprised her by asking, "Catherine, are you working now?"

Catherine sheepishly said "No," ultra-conscious of her very pregnant belly.

Before she knew it, the private reception was over and they were sitting down for coffee. After they got seated, she excused herself for a minute. Avi didn't think anything of it, as she was clearly pregnant and likely had to use the bathroom. She did just that, and then, since his back was to her, she went back to the counter and bought him one of the shop's famous cupcakes, complete with a birthday candle. She slowly brought it back to the table and wished him a happy birthday.

While he didn't know how she knew that it was his birthday, he knew right then how resourceful she was. Within minutes she was being offered the job as a product manager for his first startup, without so much as an interview or a question about her education. He told her that you could teach skills, but that the kind of intellectual curiosity and the passion for change that she had shown to him was even more important than having experience.

Avi was going to build a tech services firm that advised the travel industry on distribution technology and more specifically focused on solutions for the hospitality industry. With the advent of the Internet, so much was changing in how travel was marketed. He knew that he had resources available to him in Israel if clients wanted them to build the solutions that they were recommending.

He told Catherine, "Ultimately, I want to build a product for the hospitality industry that will shift the way consumers search for a hotel, from looking near airports and city centers to finding hotels close to venues and events. While the underlying systems that power the new online platforms don't work that way, I believe that proximity to where you are really going matters. I don't know how and I don't know when, but that is my vision. It will change the name of the game."

Catherine hadn't traveled much, but remembered when she and Andy went down to see the University of Florida, that they had to first call to find out when they had the tours. Then she had to look up the address and then figure out how long it would take to drive, or where to fly if they could afford that, and of course, what hotels were close by the university's admissions office. It had literally taken her a couple of hours to get everything set up for their trip. Consequently, his vision made complete sense to her. She was already thinking about other scenarios where the product would be useful. He told her a little bit about his early days with Hilton at his father's hotel and even his experience growing up with parents who were natural entrepreneurs.

As he was paying the bill, Avi said, "I still have a few months left at DEC, but could use your help, starting now, if you are available. I need someone to do some market research and you are perfect for that role. Although it is still confidential, DEC will likely to be sold by June. A prospective buyer is already in due diligence. I can't tell you who it is but I don't think I will be offered a job with the new firm, as they already have a strong application solutions group. I have seed capital from my parents and from the estate of my Uncle Levi, and am prepared to hire you now."

Catherine said, "Yes, absolutely!" without thinking about the implications or even asking what he would pay her.

She clearly couldn't hide that she was about to become a mother, but she was very relieved to know that he was obviously okay with it. When she questioned him about it, Avi told her that he loved children, but didn't have any of his own, at least not yet. He laughed and said, "Perhaps I can be Uncle Avi to your baby!" He told her that the word for uncle in Hebrew meant "dear one" and was used to describe the extended village that it takes to raise a child. Catherine smiled at that. She couldn't wait to go home and tell Andy. She hoped he would be as excited as she was.

What Avi said next made her smile even more. "After the DEC sale is completed and is handed over to the new team, I plan to get away from the cold weather and move to Tampa, Florida. I grew up right on the Mediterranean and one of my favorite things to do after a long day at work was to watch the sunsets over the sea."

"Avi, it is funny that you should say that, as Andy was accepted into the graduate program at the University in Tallahassee. We will leave in a few weeks after he finishes his internship at Harley Davidson. And I have to add that I share your disdain for all things snow and cold!"

"Catherine, you should be able to work from home now while Andy finishes up with Harley. Then you can work remotely in Tallahassee when you move. Eventually I would love to train you to do some consulting as well, which would require some travel. Have you ever thought about getting a nanny once the baby is born? That way you could continue to work from home, but still spend time with the baby."

Catherine's mind was running a mile a minute, her insecurities trying their hardest to break her euphoric mood. After she got home, she recounted the entire conversation with Andy as she prepared his birthday dinner.

She could see he looked a little worried. She didn't blame him, since the baby wasn't even here yet and she was already planning to go back to work.

"Avi told me about a firm that specializes in training international au pairs. Some friends of his in Tampa told him about it. I know it is hard to believe, but it is cheaper than day care in the long run for them and it has the added benefit of providing a rich cultural experience for the whole family."

Catherine waited as Andy processed what she had shared. After a very long pause, he said, "Catherine, you seemed to have forgotten your pledge to stay home for the first two years. But I must admit, the idea of you having a stable salary while I am in school and the great solution for child care has me intrigued." He smiled and she was relieved that he wasn't angry at the break of her promise. "After you get out of grad school, Avi suggested that perhaps you could get a job in Tampa. I have heard that it is beautiful." Catherine added excitedly "And the only white stuff there in the winter Andy is sand!"

It was her good fortune that Marquette University had asked Avi to speak at the event and that Andy's mother was the head of the Speaker's Bureau, as it was unlikely that their paths would ever have crossed otherwise.

Life was funny that way. Just shy of one month later they completed the move to Tallahassee.

■ ■ Tallahassee Florida | 1998–2003 Catherine ■ ■

Four months after that, Veronica had been born. The day she was born, Catherine's little sister called to congratulate her and to announced that she was pregnant. She and her husband lived right across the street from her parents, so that would make her mom very happy!

In mid 2000, after graduate school, Andy had joined a startup in Tallahassee as VP of Sales. Two of his best friends had brought in a local investor and each of the founders had put up $50,000. Catherine wondered with his degree if he should take the startup route as his first post-graduate job, but he seemed so sure that the new venture would succeed.

She was not a risk taker by nature, and reluctantly backed her husband in investing the nest egg their parents had generously given them to buy a house when they moved to Tampa.

The day that the deal closed, Andy excitedly shared with her "The founders now share 60% of the company. We only had to give up forty percent for the one-million-dollar investment by our angel, and that gave us a $2.2 million-dollar valuation!"

Catherine didn't know much about capitalization of companies, but that sounded high to her for a company that didn't have any revenues. But she knew that the guys were riding high, proud of themselves for selling their vision and getting to retain such a large piece of the company for their $150,000 investment. Of course, she knew that they had also agreed to work for the additional sweat equity by taking nominal salaries for the first year, so perhaps the investor was being generous because of that concession.

Catherine was glad that she had steady income from Avi. He was continuing to grow the value of their tech services firm and had built a strong team in Tampa. She loved being able to be home with Veronica and was grateful for their live-in au pair from Peru. That gave her the freedom to work full-time and to travel as needed, but she longed to be working side-by-side with the team in Tampa.

They were already talking about a second child, but Catherine wanted to wait a bit. Andy had said that if his business took off, that could fund their kids' educations, as well as their retirement. He was the dreamer and always thinking long term, while Catherine was looking at next week and next month. She wanted to believe, but all along, she was skeptical and she felt her dream of getting a house in Tampa slipping away.

Unfortunately, as time passed, things did not go well with Andy's company. Although the product was a great idea and it solved a very real problem, Andy wasn't successful at securing any major customers and they kept tweaking the product, to no avail. The big customer was always just one new feature away.

From the market research that she had done for Avi, Catherine knew that the "build it and they will come" philosophy didn't work, but Andy wasn't listening to her. Avi told her privately that it was a classic first time entrepreneurial mistake to focus on the product instead of the customer. Andy's group had rented high-end offices downtown and were burning through the cash as if there were no tomorrow.

In early 2001, the economy took a dive and the dot-com bust was upon them. It wasn't long before Andy's company was paying payroll with MasterCard and Visa, as the company could not get the investor to put in more money. At that point, even with the Small Business Administration programs that were available, there wasn't a bank in the State of Florida that would have given them a loan large enough to get them over the finish line.

Eighteen months after launch, they ended up shutting the doors and closing down. It was September 10, 2001, and Andy was certain that things were at rock bottom.

When he came home that day, the nanny was playing with Veronica in the living room. Living in an apartment was tight, and now that he had lost their nest egg, he didn't know how they would ever afford a house. Andy had been discouraged by the whole experience, but took advantage of the time off to enjoy spending time with their daughter. It was a good thing, as Catherine's travel was about to pick up substantially. They had been in Tallahassee much longer than originally planned. After working remotely for Avi for nearly five years, he had recently sold the tech services startup to Compaq, the company that had bought DEC years before.

Compaq was diversifying its revenues and the acquisition brought services to 25% of its total business, which increased Compaq's value substantially and provided the much-needed entry into the hospitality industry. In September 2002, Compaq was bought by Hewlett Packard for $25 billion. Catherine remembered reading that the merger was led personally by their CEO, the first woman to lead a company in the Fortune's top 20 companies. While she knew that the female CEO was ousted from HP several years later, Catherine nevertheless fantasized about being in those shoes one day.

■ ■ ■ ■

Four years after they got to Florida, Catherine and Andy started the process to adopt Connor, who at the time was two years old. They had always talked about having one of their own and adopting a child who had been orphaned. Catherine didn't want Veronica to be an only child and the timing seemed perfect.

Between January and September of that year, Catherine and Avi traveled back and forth to Houston weekly, training the Compaq team that would be leading the service group. The team included some of Avi's old compatriots from DEC and it was fun to hear some of the stories from their days together, including working with the AMR Capture team.

Even though Avi was nearly twenty-five years her senior, ever since that day that they met in Milwaukee, she had an attraction to him. She had worried about it a little at first, but now she realized that she simply admired his stability and maturity, as well as his Midas touch, and there was nothing more to it than that.

Catherine silently prayed that when they eventually moved to Tampa, Andy would get to spend more time with Avi so a little of that could rub off on him.

Avi used the proceeds from the sale to fund the current venture, to build the technology that he had described to her that day in Milwaukee that they had met. It would allow them to accomplish his dream of proximity based trip planning.

Within a few months he decided that it was time to bring Catherine to Tampa. When Avi asked Catherine and Andy to move, Andy immediately started interviewing with companies based there. It only took him a few weeks before he was invited to join the sales team with a high profile financial services company in Tampa.

The move date was set for none other than January 25. It had been nearly five years since she met Avi at Marquette. Where had the time gone?

At that time, they were still waiting for "the call" from the adoption agency to come to Vladivostok Russia to meet Connor for the first time. Until now, they had only seen the video of him when he was just over two years old, singing and smiling, despite that droopy diaper. She couldn't wait to meet him and bring him home. They should be living in Tampa by then.

"Uncle Avi" drove up to Tallahassee the week before they were to move and after spending a few hours with Veronica at the park near their apartment, he took Catherine and Andy out to dinner. They had a great time together and Catherine was grateful that Avi was there to hear Andy's story of the business failure and provide him with some advice and encouragement.

After Andy had shared his sad tale, Avi said, "Andy, you now have the most expensive piece of your education under your belt, and I'm not talking about your MBA. Every entrepreneur must meet that amazing teacher named failure before they experience true success. We have all been there." Seeing Andy's doubtful expression, Avi continued, "You may not know that a year before we sold our last company to Compaq, my partner Jonathan and I were desperately trying to find an investor. After September 11, we just didn't know how long it was going to take for the industry to rebound and whether we could hold on to see it through. Since your company had just gone under Andy, the last thing I wanted to do was worry Catherine. I will tell both of you now that there were a couple of times we weren't even sure how we were going to make payroll."

What Avi said directly to Andy next truly surprised Catherine. "There were so many dark days Andy. A little voice in my head frequently accused me of being a failure and whispered that I would never succeed in business." Catherine was certain that she was the only one who ever had such thoughts and never would have believed that "bigger than life" Avi would have even one ounce of self-doubt.

"I find that at times like these, you need to revisit the basics. Take for instance, Stephen Covey and his book, *Seven Habits of Highly Effective People*, which I now keep by my bed. One of those habits is to begin with the end in mind. My ancestors called that *keeping their eyes on the Promised Land*." Avi paused and smiled. "That is what got me through. I just had to picture what I wanted and see it in living color, in incredible detail, like an architect's drafting of a building's elevation. I knew that I was to be the CEO of a growing, well-funded business. I even envisioned the building in Tampa on the Bay where I wanted my offices to be. But in the end, it wasn't about money or things. It was about truly changing an industry, and as Max Hopper would say, *defining an era*. And I saw not just the initial product, but a whole product roadmap. And at the end of the day, I knew I didn't want to do it alone. My promised land wasn't just about business. It was about having not only my team, but someone special to share it with and leaving a legacy. Andy, just don't let your disappointment over your recent experience rob you of what is really important." He glanced quickly at Catherine and finished, "Hold on to hope and to your dreams and be grateful for those that love you and stand by your side and those that have your back."

Catherine knew he was referring to her but she couldn't help but wonder if Avi was thinking about his own situation and if he was thinking of asking his longtime girlfriend Sarah to marry him. He still had a long-distance relationship with her. She lived in Boston and worked for a travel tech startup that was trying to reinvent how attractions issued tickets. It was co-founded by a woman that she had met when she was consulting for a tour operator in Boston.

Avi had excused himself for a moment and said that he needed to make a quick phone call. Catherine wondered if he was thinking the same thing that she was.

When he returned, without skipping a beat, he went on "Entrepreneurialism isn't for everyone Andy. I'm proud of you for the job you have secured in Tampa. You are going to do very well in the financial services sector. When you get to Tampa I will introduce you to some people that may be able to help accelerate your entry into this new field. I recently met a gentleman that heads up a faith-based program called Lifework Leadership. CEOs and business owners go through a ten-month leadership training program together, spending just one day a month together. It is in Orlando, but there are many Tampa business leaders that are getting involved. Andy, I think it would be great for you on a lot of fronts and perhaps you could help them launch a Tampa chapter." Avi took out his ever-present notepad and made himself a note. "The new program starts in September. I will call Steve on Monday."

With that he turned his attention to Catherine and without any fanfare, he handed her an envelope. "Catherine, I couldn't have sold the company without your help. This should help you get settled in Tampa."

She opened the envelope with anticipation and softly gasped as she looked at the amount on the check. She had to hold back the tears as she got out of her chair and hugged Avi. The check was made out for $50,000.

■ ■ ■ ■

As Avi drove back to Tampa that night, his thoughts once again turned to the days before the purchase of his services company by Compaq. As he drove down Interstate 75, he vividly remembered the sleepless nights and the long days trying to figure out how they were going to make it if they didn't sign another client soon. His right hand, Jonathan, was always there with him, helping to evaluate their options. While he was totally open with Jonathan about their financial condition, he never, ever shared his true feelings or his fears. The stress had been crushing and his health had suffered. He should have bought stock in Glaxo Smith Kline, he had consumed so many bottles of Tums. And he was certain that he had seen every episode of *MASH*, which played on cable in the early morning hours when he couldn't sleep, kept up by his worries and his fears.

Lately, even though they had experienced early success with signing a pilot client for their new product, the pressure had returned. Although things weren't as dire as with his past company, he knew that the money they had in the bank wasn't enough to fuel the growth that he envisioned. Over the last three months he had gained weight and didn't seem to make time to start the workout that his cardiologist recommended.

His long-distance relationship with Sarah had been suffering as well. They had been dating now for more than a decade and the last time they spoke about marriage, she said that as long as he was married to his company, that she just couldn't say yes. It reminded him of the scene in his favorite holiday movie, *Scrooge* with Albert Finney, where his fiancée drops her engagement ring on a scale and then drops a few coins on the other side of the scale, showing that money was his true mistress.

While money wasn't Avi's driver, incessantly working to achieve his dream was. Working seven days a week was going to have to stop. He knew that was the root of the problem. He was addicted to getting things done, even the small unimportant things. It made him feel like he was accomplishing something.

Just yesterday, he had received a book in the mail that Sarah sent to him. It was called *Leave the Office Earlier: Do More in Less Time and Feel Great about It*. When he opened the package, he was initially angry with her. He had left her a message during dinner and hoped that she would call him back tonight. He really wanted to hear her voice and he wanted to truly thank her for sending the book. He had decided to read it and take it to heart.

As he passed the exit for Ocala, Avi thought about reducing the time that he was devoting to the company, and decided to fast track the idea of Catherine moving to Tampa. If he turned the product organization over to her, that would free up a significant amount of his time and he could then focus on the big picture of the product roadmap and building their revenues through strategic deals, rather than the minutia. It was past time for him to shift his time to work *on* the business, rather than working *in* the business.

Jonathan had recently put in a very small amount of capital, amounting to an additional one percent of equity in the company. It would get them through another two to three months. But he was concerned that it wasn't going to be enough. Jonathan had been talking to him this past week about approaching a private equity company about funding for the company. Avi had initially been resolutely against the move. He had heard so many horror stories about founders losing control of their baby. Then suddenly and without warning, Avi felt peace and clarity about the proposed strategy for their growth. He knew it was the way forward and he even had some ideas of where to start. He couldn't wait to talk to

Jonathan about it tomorrow. It was like his headlights had just switched to bright mode on a dark road.

So many of the little things that he still had on his plate could be delegated once they had funding. The thought was liberating. He also decided to contact the personal trainer that his neighbor Greg had recommended and make getting fit a priority. He knew that it would make him feel better about himself. But right this minute, his top priority was Sarah.

Just as he turned his thoughts to her, his phone rang, and it was her. He told her about his evening with Catherine and Andy and thanked her for the book and then uncharacteristically blurted out that he wanted to come to Boston for the weekend. She of course said yes, and then he told her that he had to go, but that he would explain everything when he arrived on Friday.

He knew he was too abrupt, but it was suddenly urgent for him to call Delta to secure his flights. He hoped that the next call to 1-800-Flowers would ease any anxiety that his call to Sarah may have caused. They said that the flowers would be charged to his account on file and they would be delivered by 10 a.m. the following morning. As an early adopter of all things tech, he had been using their service since they first launched on America Online in 1994, so he didn't have to give them any information other than confirming his regular order. Come to think of it, the first flowers that he had sent through their service were multi-colored roses, sent to Sarah, on the day that he realized that they were more than just business colleagues. Tomorrow, he would visit his favorite jeweler. It was time to make Sarah his bride.

Chapter 3

Desperate for Radical Collaboration

■ ■ Tampa Florida | Present | Catherine ■ ■

Catherine loved being a mom, but on the career front, time had gotten away from her. So much for the MBA. She couldn't believe that her baby was now a senior in high school and Connor had been with them for more than a decade. Her twin brother and his wife had their little boy in 2000, just two years after she and Andy left Milwaukee. So, her nephew and Connor were the same exact age. The two of them were conspiring online to attend a fishing camp in Northern Wisconsin this summer. It made her smile that they were so close. She missed her family.

Veronica was in the honor society, a student mentor, in the band, and in addition to playing soccer, she was also on the golf team. She was a great student and easily achieved an A average. She was looking forward to college in the fall and although she hadn't yet decided on which school to attend, she knew that she wanted to pursue a degree in psychology. Catherine was very proud of her.

Connor was about to turn sixteen. Good grades didn't come as easily for him as they did for his sister, and even though he was extremely smart, he just didn't test well. At the end of every single semester it was the same struggle to pull his grades up so that he wouldn't lose privileges. This semester his nemesis was Mandarin Chinese.

What Connor lacked in test grades, he more than made up in athletic ability and his winning personality. As a freshman, he was the number two seed on the varsity tennis team and a starter on the varsity football team, albeit on the special teams. He had the same number as his dad had when he played football in high school. Number 8. Connor's grandfather had gotten his letter in tennis in high school and never missed any of Connor's matches. Her parents were even able to watch him play football, as his high school had a broadcast team, so they could watch it live or on demand. And during basketball season, Connor was trying his hand at calling the plays during the game, so they even watched those games. '

Andy's parents had moved to Tampa last year when his dad received an assignment at MacDill Airforce Base. Connor loved hearing about his granddad's military experiences, and after graduation, Connor talked about applying for the ROTC program at Stetson University, as he felt strongly about supporting the country with his service. But he also wanted to pursue a degree in Marine Biology, as a foundation for his goal of having a fishing show on television. It was the perfect match for his talents. He was an outstanding fisherman and he never gave up on anything. She loved that about him and she knew that he would accomplish his dream, no matter which direction he ultimately chose.

To reduce the stress in her life, Catherine tried to keep her eyes on the big picture with the kids' education, but it was increasingly difficult with the school's grading system which sent text messages every time a grade was posted. She longed for the good old days when you only brought home a paper report card once a semester. It was less pressure on everyone!

■ ■ ■ ■ ■

Catherine had just gotten back to the office after the ill-fated offsite and couldn't help but think back on her early days as a product manager. She had grown significantly professionally and was now leading Marketing and Product Management. They called it Product Innovation.

She was amazed when they moved to Tampa in 2002 that Avi had given up owning the product, but she had to admit that she not only loved her job, but she had been told that she was a natural!

Avi had made good on his promise to Andy to introduce him to some key people in the community. Andy had been in the class of 2003-2004 for Lifework Leadership. He was now active in their alumni group and he even volunteered each year, assisting with facilitation of the table groups for the monthly meetings. He made great connections for business and they had some amazing speakers.

A few years ago, they had a female executive that shared her story, which included investing in textiles, which included buying a collection of Princess Diana's gowns, just before her death. Andy knew how much Catherine had loved Princess Diana and he had been excited to tell her about it when he got home that day. Catherine couldn't remember her name, but she knew that she was involved somehow with the University of Tampa, which is where they held the Lifework Leadership classes.

Andy was doing well, but his income was volatile, based largely on commissions. When she looked at their combined income, she never understood how they couldn't seem to save more. Having access to long-term financial planning services as a part of Andy's benefits was a comfort, but due to the impact of the economic crisis a few years ago coupled with the startup debacle, their savings were a bit thinner than they hoped they would be seventeen years into their marriage.

Catherine was concerned about the future. They had talked many times about the Florida pre-paid education program to pay for college for the kids, but had never made it a priority in their budget. Now with two teens headed to college, Catherine was nervous, but she knew that she just had to keep the faith.

Her daughter's soccer team was in first place in their division. Last year they had taken the State championship. Playing in the Florida Youth Soccer League, in addition to playing on her school's team, had been important for her college application process, as they were hoping she would be eligible for a sports scholarship. They should be hearing any day now. Veronica had always been a good student, but the advanced placement classes last year were more challenging than she had expected and she was clearly worried about the SAT tests. All of that added together meant that they might not be able to depend on an academic scholarship.

The bottom line was that she and Andy wanted the very best for their kids. Yet Catherine was sad that without a scholarship, they wouldn't have the money saved to send Veronica to the university that was her first choice.

Veronica had started looking at schools in Europe, as many of them were much more affordable. Strangely, the University of Warsaw was at the top of her list right now. Catherine tried not to think about what it would be like to have her baby so far away. She secretly believed it would be good for she and her boyfriend Andrew to go to separate schools, but had never dreamed that Veronica would choose to go to school abroad.

Their decision to send both kids to a private high school had been a huge drain on their monthly budget, but she and Andy agreed that the college-prep focus and the faith-based worldview was a long-term investment in the lives of their kids and worth the sacrifice.

Their son, Connor, still had three years before he would graduate and that provided a little time before they had to worry about college for him. He was a natural athlete and never met a sport he didn't like. Thankfully a sports scholarship was much more likely to be in the cards for him. Connor was a diehard 49ers fan, and although he had already settled on his desired career, he still fantasized about playing professional football.

Andy had grown up in Fond du Lac, Wisconsin, next door to Rick and Theresa Kaepernick. In the mid-80s, Rick and Theresa tragically lost two babies to heart disease. During the time that they were grieving their loss, even though Rick was ten years older than Andy, he and Rick became best friends, shooting hoops, watching football and anything else that Andy could think to do to distract Rick.

In 1987 when they adopted their son Colin, they named Andy as his godfather. A few years later, they moved to California, but Rick and Andy had stayed in touch. Now, in honor of his best friend, Andy had left his beloved Packers behind in favor of the 49ers, as Colin had gone there as their quarterback.

A few years ago, when the Tampa Bay Bucs had played the 49ers, Colin had arranged for tickets on the 50-yard line for the whole family. Connor had been beside himself to not only see his favorite team, but to meet his personal hero. Even Veronica thought it was cool that his dad had grown up in the same town with the 49ers quarterback.

Last season, Colin made a polarizing decision that rocked their family, when he refused to stand during the National Anthem at the pre-season games. The move was meant to call attention to racial injustice and police brutality. Although Colin's birth mother was white, his birth father had been black and Colin had decided to take a stand against all the recent violence.

Just after that event, she and Andy had to have a long discussion with Connor about Colin's first amendment right to freedom of speech. When he got home from school that next day, Connor had announced that he was using Colin as the central character in his English paper on heroes. While they understood why, they couldn't remain silent on the bigger picture.

Andy told Connor "Son, while you can say or do anything that doesn't directly harm others and not go to jail, you don't get to choose the social consequences." Twitter had been ablaze with blowback from fans, and even Colin's birth mom had chimed in with her disappointment in him. Catherine interjected "You know Connor, Colin's parents, Rick and Theresa, declined to comment to the media. I think that was wise." Andy added, "This is so hard for them. Colin is a role model not just for you, Connor, but for kids all over the country."

The next game Colin had softened his position a bit by kneeling during the anthem, instead of standing. Ironically it had been "Salute to the Military" night at the Charger game. At half-time after the crowd had spent so much time booing Connor's hero, they also talked as a family about what the flag and the national anthem represented. Catherine reminded Connor of their own flagpole that grandpa had helped Andy and Connor install last year, complete with the spotlight, so they could fly the flag twenty-four hours a day in honor of the country that they loved. "Connor, remember the day that we put up the flag for the first time, we talked about the hard-won freedom that the flag represented. One of those freedoms was what gives you, and Colin the ability to express your frustrations."

Last summer Connor had insisted on flying it at half-mast when the police were killed in Dallas, so he was confused when he saw the picture of Colin on the Internet, wearing socks that depicted the police as pigs. She was proud of Connor for his recognition of the conflict, but sad that it had to involve him questioning the decision of his family friend and hero.

And just today she heard that the 49ers had let Kaepernick go and he was now a free agent. She guessed they would have another talk tonight at dinner. She wondered whether his loyalty would stay with the 49ers or go with Colin wherever he landed.

Catherine's reverie was broken by the sound of a text.

Andy and Connor had arrived at Tampa University and Veronica's team was ahead three to one at the half. Attached was a picture, which she assumed was her daughter scoring a goal. It was going to be a good night after all. If Catherine left now, she might make it to the Culvers restaurant on Hillsborough Avenue in Tampa, just a mile or so from their house. It had opened a few years ago and although Veronica had recently gotten a job there, Catherine had yet to try it out, at least not here in Tampa.

It had been one of her favorites when she lived in Milwaukee. They were known for their many flavors of frozen custard, but that didn't quite fit in with her Kilimanjaro training regime. The girls were going there for custard after the game. With any luck, it would be a celebration. If they won today, the team would go on to the regional championships for their travel league.

She couldn't wait to see her daughter. Veronica had still been in bed when she left for the gym at 5:30 a.m., not unusual for a teenager! She had been up late, talking online with her boyfriend, Andrew, alternatively studying and playing some group online game with his friends. He was a really solid student and a great guy, so, as long as her grades were up, Catherine and Andy didn't worry about the late-night game fests. She paused from her busy thoughts and wondered whether Veronica and Andrew would eventually get married, and someday look back and also tell the story of being high school sweethearts. Andrew's mom, Sierra, was absolutely certain that this would be the case, as Veronica was such a perfect fit for her son.

Sierra and Catherine were the same age and Catherine enjoyed their time together. Sierra was completely and totally passionate about personality types, but her day job was as the owner of a boutique. Sierra was very creative and it showed in everything she did. Catherine had enjoyed having Sierra explore personality types with her, as well as understanding why Veronica and Andrew were so well suited. Catherine was a clear ENTJ on the Myers Briggs™ scale, as extroverted as they came, fully using her intuition to take in information. Her hero Margaret Thatcher was one of the most famous ENTJs.

Catherine was a thinker, which contrasted to Sierra's feeling approach to life. Catherine liked order and rules, and while the "J" stood for judging, she was anything but. Of course, when she would say that, Sierra always reminded her that judging didn't mean judgmental, but instead represented the way information is processed and fully informed decisions were made. When they got together last week, Catherine had asked her if she would be willing to come in and use the MBTI instrument with her team. Catherine knew that it would help them to better understand one another and to more productively collaborate on the product.

Catherine packed up her bag, carefully inserting her laptop into its designated slot and rolling up her power cord, as she had to get some work done tonight after the kids were in bed. She couldn't remember the last time that she and Andy had actually gone to bed at the same time when he was in town. She had mastered walking through the bedroom in the dark using her phone as illumination so that she wouldn't wake him up. She had to admit though, that this was getting old. It was tough to keep the magic in their marriage without making time for intimacy.

All day meetings were the norm now, from conference room to conference room, each one ending with everyone pulling out their smartphones to access their calendars to set the next meeting. Didn't they see the futility? Sometimes they behaved like a company of ten thousand employees, versus being a team of twenty-five. When would they ever have time to actually do the work that they talked about all day? She fantasized about locking all of the conference rooms and throwing away the keys, and chuckled to herself at the panic that would ensue. *Sometimes I think we just have meetings because the conference rooms overlooked the Bay. No doubt, it was beautiful,* she thought.

■ ■ ■ ■

The meetings that she had attended for the last three days had turned out to be more than tedious. It was sad really, as she had been looking forward to the offsite strategic planning session. In the past, these types of meetings had been really energizing and the team usually ended on a high, with at least one big, new idea that could change the face of the company or even their industry—that seed of innovation that had attracted her to Avi that day back in 1998.

This time, the facilitator was horrible and each time Catherine tried to introduce something even remotely innovative, her ideas were summarily shot down and the facilitator did nothing to stop it. It had started on the first day when Catherine had jumped in at the structured brainstorming session. She had said, "I would love to see a Google Calendar plug-in added to our product line!" Jake, their CFO, asked Catherine, "What is a plug-in?"

Avi didn't allow Catherine to answer Jake, but instead brushed her idea aside, "No, no, no! We need to look at integrating our tools into SalesForce.com as a priority, that would give us much faster penetration with the business traveler, since so many companies use their tools to track their prospects and client activity online."

She knew it was a waste of time to remind him that he had turned over product management to her, or to jog his mind about the targeting work they had done the past month with the sales analytics company. In that facilitated session, they had agreed to target "Laura, the do-it-all location manager" for their launch of the new travel widget product, not "Ryan, the frequent business traveler." Laura and Ryan were two of the personas that they had developed in a marketing workshop that signified the key characteristics of their various target audiences.

By now, after working with Avi for so many years, she was used to him putting his ideas at the top of the queue and unraveling planning work that they were doing with their partners. But by the end of day three, she felt like

© marketoonist.com

she was the main character in the Tom Fishburne cartoon on brainstorming that she recently received in her *Marketoonist* subscription. It was always the highlight of her week, but she nearly missed the cartoon in the two hundred plus emails that she had to plow through daily. *My email is totally out of control,* she thought.

Yet, even with the disastrous brainstorming session, something deep inside her told her that this year was going to be different. *It just had to be!*

Despite his "shiny object syndrome" behavior, she did love working with Avi. Even though he was now in his mid-sixties, he was so energetic that she sometimes forgot that she hadn't even been born when he immigrated to the U.S.

■ ■ 2004 | Boston | Avi and Jonathan ■ ■

Back in 2004 when he had decided to raise money, Avi and Jonathan had done some research on their different choices for funding. The first call he had made was to his friend Benjamin, who was at the time, the Minister of Finance in Israel. He had worked with Boston Consulting Group when he graduated from MIT. Avi knew he had made some great connections in the investment community when he was there. Benjamin was gracious enough to take time out of his busy schedule to make some referrals on the funding front, including some prominent private equity companies and venture capital (VC) firms in both New York and Boston. Avi was grateful for the introductions, but at the end of their research, they found that it was a little too early in the company's growth to go the private equity or VC route and they made the decision to raise money with an angel investor.

After getting counsel from Jody, their corporate attorney, they decided to use a Private Placement Memorandum (PPM), and rather than giving up equity at the outset, they chose a Convertible Note, repayable in three years. That was just a fancy term for a loan, but it had a unique characteristic that the person loaning the money had the option of converting the debt to equity, versus being repaid in full plus the interest. Avi felt like it would defer the decision to give up control and that was appealing.

As it turned out, they found an angel investor in Tampa that loaned them the money that they were seeking. But they quickly found out that the notion of retaining control was just an illusion.

Avi felt naïve and a tad sick to his stomach when he realized that he didn't have the final say anymore. The operating agreement for the company said that he did, but that didn't seem to matter to the investor when they had their regular progress reviews, which were all too frequent for Avi's taste. In retrospect, he realized that he did not like having his decisions questioned. Fortunately, that was balanced out by the incredible support and mentoring that he got from the investor, who had become a personal friend through the whole experience.

Avi and the team worked really hard over the next three years to grow the company's revenues and pay off the full amount that they borrowed, with interest. He had decided that even if they had to bootstrap the company moving forward, that he wanted to do everything possible to retain control.

Even though Avi was masterful at managing money, right after paying off the note, the economic downturn hit and growth was much slower than he had hoped.

By 2014, Avi had to swallow his pride and look outside for capital again. Despite the road bumps on the previous venture, he was thankful that Jody was still one of his key advisors and believed in him and his vision.

Thank God for my "village."

■ ■ Tampa | Present Day | Catherine ■ ■

Catherine observed in the meeting today that the last decade of bootstrapping the company had taken a toll on Avi. The company had finally gotten funded last spring by a private equity firm shortly after her promotion to vice president. They referred to their benefactors lovingly as *The Firm*, reminiscent of the 1991 book by John Grisham. It wasn't that this Firm was sinister as in the book, it was that they were just not in control of their own destiny any more, now that they had accepted outside funding. This was par for the course and they had to remind themselves of where they would be without the investment. Where the focus used to be long-term innovation, now the emphasis was on quarter-to-quarter profits, which Catherine knew had stifled their creativity.

Catherine missed the days when Avi talked incessantly to the team about his hero Max Hopper. She was reminded of his fascination with him during the offsite when they were reviewing the project planning organization that fell under Catherine's leadership. Avi had recounted a story involving his hero. She remembered hearing some of the same story the day they had met. But in the retelling, this time the passion was gone.

The entrepreneurial spirit that had attracted her to Avi over sixteen years ago that day at the Marquette lecture was a distant memory. Avi had changed. Even after the acquisition and having the money to grow the business, he was looking every day of his sixty-five years. She thought, *Rather than seeing the funding as a success, Avi seems to treat it as a failure. I find that curious.*

The only bright spot for Catherine was Amanda, the extraordinary partner from the Firm. When they met, in spite of the nearly fifteen-year difference in their ages, Amanda had taken an immediate interest in Catherine and offered to mentor her. She loved their time together when Amanda flew in to Tampa from New York, where the headquarters of Firm was located. She hoped that Avi didn't mind the time that Amanda spent with her and set a mental reminder. *I need to ask him the next time we have our one-on-one session if my relationship with Amanda troubles him at all.*

From time to time, and especially on days like today when she didn't feel "educated enough," she found herself wondering what would have happened if she had finished her MBA. She had even asked Amanda in their last session, "Would I be a Senior Vice President by now had I not given up the graduate degree program for motherhood?"

Rather than answering her question directly, like the great mentor that she was, Amanda said, "Let's look at Executive MBA programs for you after you get back from your climb in Africa." Catherine enthusiastically responded, "What a great idea! I have heard a lot of good things about those programs and I've even looked into the one right here at the University of Tampa." Amanda echoed her sentiments and suggested that they schedule a visit to the campus soon.

Amanda added, "In fact, one of my dear friends, Maureen Daly, was the first and only woman to chair the board of trustees at UT. Just a few months ago one of the buildings on the campus was named after her. It houses the Entrepreneurship Center. You will love hearing her amazing story. At one time, she owned a collection of Princess Diana's dresses, and she has overcome a lot of adversity in her life. It is a real testament to her faith."

Catherine jumped in and said, "Oh yes Andy heard her speak a few years ago at a program that he is involved with, and then about five years ago Andy surprised me and took me to Downtown Disney to see the dress collection exhibition. Small world!"

Amanda laughed. "Yes, it is at that! I will get in touch with Maureen and see if she has any connections in the Executive MBA program. Perhaps we can even make the program work this year, since your climb is in October after the program will have already begun."

Catherine shared, "All through high school I idolized Princess Diana. When I was just a toddler, one of my earliest memories was seeing her wedding on TV. Actually, I was just a baby, so I'm not sure how that is even possible! When I was three my parents gave me a doll that looked just like her. I think I still have it in a box in the attic! It will be incredible to hear Maureen's story! And, one of my favorite restaurants is right across the street from UT. We'll have to go there for lunch after the tour. You will love it. It has a specialty tea bar with hundreds of teas, a bookstore, and a very cool gift boutique."

Amanda immediately agreed and said, "We will schedule it on one of my upcoming trips back to Tampa. I should know my schedule in the next few days."

Imagine that, I may get an Executive MBA from UT and meet the former owner of the Diana dress collection! I can't wait to tell Andy.

She had been so busy in her work and personal life that the possibility of an Executive MBA program had not occurred to her. She could hardly believe that this could be a reality.

I really can have it all!

She recalled a conversation yesterday with Sierra. "In the past, Avi was always positive, even in the face of competition, market pressures or the economic crisis they had survived. He supported me in my desire to get training, but the Company doesn't have any money for such luxuries right now. I have relied mostly on online programs and seeking out mentors."

That was how Catherine found the Executive Girlfriends' Group. The group normally allowed only C-level executives (those that were CEOs or reported to one) and entrepreneurs as members, but Catherine had gotten in on a special program called NextGen Leaders. Catherine shared with Sierra, "I love the woman that heads up the program. Cecilia founded her own technology company in the Boston area in 2003. Oddly enough, Avi's wife Sarah was a part of her start up team. Small world. And just two years later Cecilia was named to the Boston Business Journal's, 'Top 40 Executives Under 40.'"

Spending time with the women's group on the phone each Friday for their one-hour call had become an inviolate entry on Catherine's calendar. Even Avi knew that she would not miss that call unless it was a dire emergency.

These days, Avi always had a harried look on his face, and the weeks leading up to a board meeting were non-stop fire drills with endless research and analysis. She was starting to really hate creating those presentation decks. The budget exercise had expanded from a couple of days per year to where it was now swallowing up nearly two full months.

Can't Avi and Amanda see what a waste of time it is? I'll bet Jake is the culprit.

The extended focus on budgeting and strategic planning began when their new CFO arrived on the scene from the Firm. Before Jake, Avi just had a part-time bookkeeper who had worked with their CPA. There was no controller in the company. That wasn't unusual for early stage companies.

She wistfully remembered how she felt on the morning just eighteen short months ago when she was promoted to Vice President of Product Innovation, responsible for product marketing, product management and development. On that day, Avi walked into her office with his signature Starbucks cup in his hand and sat on the couch in her office by the window. "Catherine, I think it is time." Catherine had looked quickly at her calendar, wondering if she was late for something. "What did I miss, Avi?" He handed her a box, which she had not seen when he walked in, and excitedly said, "Open it!" Catherine took off the cover of the beautiful navy blue linen box and gasped as she saw a new nameplate for her door: Catherine Cousins, Vice President.

She could only describe her reaction as pure, unadulterated joy.

After the investment by the Firm which occurred shortly after her promotion, all evidence of that joy was gone and her relationship with Avi had changed. He rarely ever came to her office anymore. He seemed to always be tied up with Jake, behind closed doors. Avi had aged a decade since the purchase. Although he was nearing sixty-five, he had always seemed much younger to Catherine. He attributed that to his young children. They were a product of his second marriage to Sarah.

Now Catherine found herself yearning for the days in the previous venture when Avi drove them all crazy with his "idea a minute" style. It was exhausting, but energizing. She laughed wryly as she realized that the joy that she experienced that day was a distant memory, lost in the drudgery of interminable meetings.

Joy. I wonder if I will ever relate that word to my work again? She had just seen a notice on her timeline on Facebook about a radio show interview from her women's group. The show would include an interview with Rich Sheridan, the author of *Joy, Inc. I'll have to make sure to RSVP to that one!*

She now spent her days managing dozens of pointless projects where she was directed to add incremental features to tired old products. The Product Innovation group name itself was a joke. The only bright spot was the partnership that Avi had formed with their development firm. Catherine so loved working with Joe, their Senior Vice President of Service Delivery, who coincidentally, lived in the same neighborhood as she and Andy. The relationship seemed destined to be and Catherine knew that if she could get the approval to move ahead with some of her ideas, that their development partner would be ready and able to step up. But for now, she wasn't going to hold her breath.

Press releases were timed now to coincide with board meetings, versus heralding truly game changing products and services, as they had done in the early days when she was the Product Manager. She had recently hired a new Product Manager. She had worked for their design firm, Multiplica, heading up product design and development for their Latin American division. *Maybe she can help me push forward the Spanish language version of the product for the millions of Hispanics in the US! I can dream anyway.*

She yearned for the excitement that she felt each time that she received her issue of *Fast Company* magazine, the one publication that she still received in hard copy. She even dreamed about being on the cover one day as the, "Young CEO that has Silicon Valley buzzing." But that wasn't happening anytime soon. She had barely mastered her current role and she knew that she was not the heir apparent to the throne.

She had thought Jonathan, Avi's right hand was slated for that but he had just been moved to sales; and Tim, the VP of Sales was promoted to SVP of Customer Service. They had never clicked.

I pray that Tim isn't being groomed for Avi's role. He always seems so smug and superior. Perhaps if I get the Executive MBA I will at least be considered for the SVP role. We sure could use the extra money. College was looming and Andy's income fluctuated so much each month. It was a constant worry.

It was all that she could do to keep up with her day-to-day responsibilities, let alone work on creating a game-changing product that anyone would want to buzz about. She didn't even have the energy to get excited about anything that they were presently working on.

The Company's product line was stale. Catherine had products that were crying out to be retired, long bypassed by the offerings of their competitors. It seemed that everything in their current plan was barely moving the needle. The new dashboard that they were using to guide the team reflected just that.

Jonathan, the new VP of sales, and her longtime colleague from Avi's first venture was single and could devote so much more time to his role with the Company. Even though she loved her family, she sometimes wistfully remembered the simplicity of the very early days in her career before Veronica was born, when Andy was still in school and she only had to worry about herself. Balancing the twelve-hour workdays was physically and emotionally draining. Add to that, her responsibilities as mom and wife, plus training for the climb and life was quickly escalating to overwhelming.

She mused on her decision to make the climb of the tallest freestanding peak in the world. She had been told by those that had gone before her that this would be the toughest thing that she would do, ever. Every spare moment that she was not working or dashing to sporting events was spent training. The climb was just six months away.

I am getting stronger, but I'm not anywhere near ready. Catherine tried to remember the last time she ever spent time with friends. That was a luxury that she couldn't afford right now.

What has happened to me? I didn't sign up for this.

As Catherine walked to her car, her smart phone beeped with a notification, which she ignored. She put her things in the back seat and plugged in her phone to charge on the way to the restaurant. It seemed like the battery life was getting shorter and shorter by the day.

She missed Steve Jobs and the focus on quality that he had brought to the Apple products that she had been buying for more than two decades. She didn't understand how they had just achieved a market cap of nearly seven hundred billion dollars, more than twice that of Microsoft, when quality continued to slip. Yet, Apple had recently posted the largest earnings of any company on the globe. It just didn't make sense to her.

Her products might be stale, but they were solid; yet the Company certainly hadn't commanded a large market cap when the investor had come in. Disappointing really. Admittedly, the finer points of finance had always escaped her. *It is like I have a mental block when it comes to numbers. Perhaps it is because*

I am a creative. She sometimes joked with her husband that she was number phobic, not able to keep up with the rest of the team when they reviewed the Company's results each quarter. No worries—the Executive MBA would no doubt fix that!

It would take her about forty-five minutes to get to Culvers at this time of day. Traffic had gotten much worse in the decade since they moved to Tampa. The phone beeped again and after audibly saying, "What now?" she decided just to check it before she got on the road so she wouldn't be further distracted, thinking about who was trying to get ahold of her. *It is probably Andy or Veronica.*

It was there again. A notification of a radio show on innovation and growth that she had seen yesterday. But after getting shot down more times than she could remember in the meeting yesterday, she really hadn't been up to listening. The show was being rebroadcast from last Friday. She had missed the show due to the offsite meeting. She had promised herself that she would go back and listen to the show on iTunes, but she hadn't quite gotten around to it. There was always something more pressing. Her life seemed to be guided these days by the tyranny of the urgent. Investing time in her own growth generally took the back seat and she was now feeling the effects of that self-neglect.

The show aired on BlogTalkRadio, an internet-based radio network, so she knew that she could always go back and listen at another time. This time the host was interviewing the author of a book called *The Improvisation Edge*, by Karen Hough (pronounced "Huff"). With a forty-five minute drive ahead of her, she decided to ditch her normal talk radio station and listen to the interview. *It is time to invest some time in me.*

The funny thing is that the email said that the show had originally aired in 2011. She had thought it was the program from last Friday.

Either my iTunes subscription has gone haywire or someone really wants me to hear this show.

She synched her phone with the Bluetooth system in her car and began listening. In the first twenty seconds of the show, it grabbed her. The host said that the book, written by a former performer with Second City in Chicago, was about building trust and radical collaboration at work. *It has been a long time since I experienced either of those things at work.* It was true. She didn't feel like anyone trusted her instincts anymore.

Unless you could research it and write a business case for it, with our new owners it just didn't get done. Forget knowing in your gut that something will really work or planting seeds of innovation and nurturing them. And radical collaboration? Ha!

As those thoughts traveled through Catherine's mind, she heard Karen the author say to the show's host, "Did you ever want to do something completely different?"

Right then she knew that unless she could find those things in her own circumstances within her current job, as much as it pained her to abandon Avi, it was time to start thinking about formulating her Plan B.

The author continued, "My background is in improvisational theatre. Improvisers must work in an environment of trust. Improvisation, by its nature, is one of the riskiest, most uncertain fields of performance. It requires a group of performers to create a scene, game or play without a script." Catherine had to laugh. That sounded like the first venture with Avi and Jonathan!

The interviewer then asked the author what she meant and clearly wasn't familiar with improv theatre. Catherine actually loved the genre and had been to Second City about a decade ago when she went back to Chicago to see her college roommate.

■ ■ ■ ■

Catherine was brought back to the moment again. The author answered the interviewer with a smile in her voice, "We don't really know what our troupe members will say or do from moment to moment, yet we are able to create incredible shows on the fly. Every improviser relies on her partners, her audience and her own ability to listen and change to create something, under pressure, in every performance."

Catherine was starting to see how much improv and product management had in common!

Catherine turned her attention back to the author, pressing the audio back button on her steering wheel to make sure she didn't miss anything. *I love Bluetooth and the freedom that it gives me in the car.*

"Improv has a clear set of guidelines. Improvisers practice and work at their craft like crazy. Improvisers trust their troupe members implicitly. Really brilliant improv is about finding the least obvious, most surprising outcome in any situation."

That made a lot of sense, especially since she had experienced it herself firsthand as an improvisational audience member. She found herself wondering if Karen, the author, had been the rutabaga onstage when she had seen Second City a decade ago? Her voice sounded strangely familiar. She had loved how that night the troupe had turned around the situation when a member of the audience had gotten upset over the use of sign language, apparently done badly, and how they had actually convinced her to stay and take part in the skit by doing American Sign Language to properly translate the wacky vegetable skit.

Karen the author was giving out her email address and her website address. Since Catherine was driving, she couldn't write it down, but when she got to the restaurant, she would just go ahead and order the book on Amazon. Maybe she'd even write to her to see if she could help their team break out of their product slump!

As the radio show ended, she wondered if there was anywhere in Tampa where she could take her team to see an improv show. *Perhaps it isn't too late to learn more about the guidelines for improvisational success and how it could help us get the Company back on track.*

Chapter 4

Understanding the Law of Value

■ ■ Boston | 1974 | Jonathan ■ ■

They had met in Boston when Avi was attending MIT. Jonathan had come to Boston on a summer school exchange program in 1974 from the UK. He had grown up in a small town on the Bristol Channel in Somerset, England. He had the good fortune to be accepted into a special graduate summer school session at Harvard for entrepreneurs, even though he was just an undergrad at the University of Manchester. It helped that his dad knew the head of the program. He was a Brit.

Being on the Seagulls football (a.k.a. soccer) team for the past six years had been a boon as well, as they were looking for athletes as well as scholars for the program, unusual for Harvard, but no doubt a result of his dad's mate's love of football. Jonathan had dreamed in those days of one day being on the Manchester United Football team and playing in the World Cup. It was his one passion in life.

He would never forget the day that their friendship deepened, nearly forty-two years ago. They were classmates in the summer session. The date was August 9, 1974 and Avi had called him, noticeably upset, mumbling something about Richard Nixon. As a Brit, Jonathan hadn't been caught up in the Watergate hearings like his American friends, but he had heard that he had resigned the presidency. Avi was running off to meet with his advisor to sign up for a new class for the fall.

That night they met at the pub halfway between MIT and Harvard and toasted to ethics—more than once, although truth be known, the memory of that night was a tad foggy.

■ ■ Tampa | Present Day | Jonathan, VP of Sales ■ ■

For the better part of the last decade Jonathan had been the head of Customer Service, responsible for operations and all customer interaction for Avi's various companies. He was by Avi's side when he founded the current firm, as well as with his first startup that they sold to Compaq. Jonathan was cautious by nature, which suited his partnership with Avi, his crazy, innovative friend and colleague. They balanced one another.

Where Avi was passionate about simply everything and often jumped in just based on what his gut was telling him, Jonathan was the analytical one, dotting all the i's and crossing all the t's. On their initial encounter, they were working on a business case study and Avi was glad that Jonathan was on his team, as he didn't have the patience for detailed analysis.

Even though they had been struggling financially over the last few years, the Company had made it through the economic crisis, but just barely. Jonathan and Avi had recently decided that the only way forward was to take in outside investment, something that they had resisted for a long time. They had a bad experience with an angel investor a few years ago.

Avi had put up all of the funding for the business from the sale of his last venture, but without Jonathan's help to provide the infrastructure for the company and the discipline to deliver the product and service the customers, they never would have gotten off the ground. Jonathan was the fuel to Avi's rocket.

Avi was brilliant and really skilled at managing money. Jonathan loved working with him, but left to his own devices, time had proven that Avi couldn't execute his way out of a paper bag.

When the private equity group came in, the partner from the Firm did a swap of Jonathan's position with Tim, the VP of Sales, taking on his old role and now Jonathan was heading up the global sales team. To add insult to injury, since Tim had his MBA, Jake, the new Chief Financial Officer, who also conveniently headed up human resources, had elevated Jonathan's old position to make Tim an SVP. *It just wasn't fair. Tim wasn't even thirty years old!*

■ ■ ■ ■

This was Jonathan's worst nightmare. He would have gone to Avi, but it was clear that while he still had the CEO title, that he was no longer calling the shots. It was funny how quickly things had changed.

When Jonathan got the news, he was completely gutted by it and stayed home under the guise of being sick. But what was really happening behind the scenes was that he simply couldn't face his fear and the pressure of his new role. Operations and Customer Service came naturally to him. They were as effortless to him as breathing. Jonathan thought, *even swapping with Catherine would have been tolerable, as Lord knows that I love the product side of things. But sales? Really? Sales required personality and creativity. When those things were handed out, I was clearly in a different line. Now what?*

Jonathan knew how to lead, but truly didn't know the first thing about how to do all the things Tim had talked about from his world: decision makers, budget holders, influencers, and stakeholders. The sales discipline was clearly a science and he had not studied it nor did he ever have an interest in it. But he did love customers.

After three days of binge watching five seasons of the *True Blood* series from HBO, Jonathan made a decision. *I don't have to like my new job, but I do have to do it. Avi is counting on me and I won't tread lightly into this new challenge.*

So, he returned to work, humming the *True Blood* theme song. Jonathan dove in with the same dedication that he had given the company since it was founded. *I will find a way to learn about sales and make sure the sales team succeeded. I owe that to Avi.*

As he drove to the office he thought about his love for football (aka soccer). He still loved the sport, but now rather than wanting to play in the World Cup, his goal was to get them as a client of their new technology to make it easier for fans to attend matches around the world. It was a long shot, but he was bound and determined.

The truth of the matter was that he had not had a high regard for the sales part of the organization since Tim took over eighteen months ago. His people over-promised and sold things that Catherine's group hadn't even finished designing. More often than not, they discounted everything just to get the deal, resulting in the decline in profitability. And now, Jonathan was taking over the mess that Tim left behind.

The pressure was on from the investment firm. Profits for the second quarter were down and all eyes were on the sales team for an explanation. Jonathan

had watched service decline since Tim took over and was already battling the argument from his sales people that no one was willing to pay full price. It was a vicious circle.

Jonathan was feeling like the man in the cartoon that he had received just this morning in his email. Catherine had turned him on to the *Marketoonist* a few weeks ago and he was enjoying the tongue in cheek, clever approach that Tom Fishburne used in his work. It suited his sense of humor.

Fishburne says things in his cartoons that most of us just think but would never say out loud!

The strategy session over the last three days didn't shed much light on how he was going to turn things around in his organization. The facilitator seemed to just pander to the board members that were in the session, versus really caring about getting a strategy in place that would work. At one point, Jonathan had asked him, "Would you explain your process to get us from the brainstorming to the strategy?" The facilitator had actually had the gall to say, "You are just going to have to trust that because the Firm has hired me, the process works."

The methods that the facilitator used could have been taken directly out of a textbook. It was truly painful to watch. Dysfunction was rampant and Jonathan was gobsmacked that no one did anything about it.

The old Avi would have thrown this guy out on day one. We need to create an executable plan, developed in an integrated fashion across the Company. We can't rely on theory. Isolated budget exercises, particularly with the likelihood of more staff cuts, are just not a path to growth.

Truth be known, while he was very detailed oriented, Jonathan didn't really understand finance. His spreadsheet skills were barely passable. He was grateful that Jake, their CFO, provided templates to the executive team to use for the creating their budgets, but he could see that he would need some help with modeling sales deals, as every client's metrics were slightly different. *Perhaps I can talk to Catherine about building a tool to predict client revenues from the deal terms.*

Jonathan didn't have an MBA like Tim did, but he didn't want anyone to know that he didn't understand what was being said when the discussion turned to the company's financial results. He knew that Catherine struggled a bit as well on the finance front. He hoped Jake and Amanda didn't notice his discomfort.

Last week, Catherine had come into Jonathan's office unannounced, saying, "Can you believe that Tim got the promotion to SVP? We both have a decade more of experience than he does!" She was upset and he knew why.

"I know Catherine. While he was learning about business, we were building two businesses with Avi."

While they both knew they shouldn't care about titles, the fact is that they did. Titles gave the outside world a signal of responsibility and relative value to the company. Jonathan was extremely comfortable with the product side of things and had a keen eye for the direction that he thought they should take. It was an important part of the operations and service side of the business.

He had sensed Catherine's frustration in the meeting today, as all of the ideas she put on the table were shot down. He was a little surprised that Avi had been the one to derail her first and that he chimed in each time Tim put her ideas down. It was like a bad movie. Jonathan had wanted to say something about the decline in service quality, but he was afraid that it would be taken as criticism of his colleague and a veiled excuse for the poor sales numbers this quarter.

He could tell that Tim was feeling the pressure too. Jake had asked him today, "Tim, what is happening with the customer call answering time? We have seen calls stay on hold longer and longer over the last three weeks and our lost call volume is up by twenty five percent. This is not the way we want this KPI to go."

Jonathan knew that KPI meant key performance indicator, but it seemed like Tim was caught off-guard, as he definitely did not have the answer. He simply said, "Don't worry Jake, I have it under control!" It reminded Jonathan of the silly Bobby McFerrin song, "Don't worry, be happy." The song and the incessant whistling began playing in his head, distracting him from the conversation. He struggled to get re-engaged after that.

A part of Jonathan felt sorry for Tim. He was definitely a fish out of water and he knew from comments made by his own former team members that they were not happy about the executive swap. *It is bloody tough to succeed in a leadership role when your team does not support you,* Jonathan thought.

Jonathan was tired, but didn't want to go home to his empty apartment. All of his colleagues were married and had families to go home to. While being single sounded like a great idea, especially when he bragged about his freedom to the mates he hung out with at the local British pub, he really longed for the solid relationships his friends had with their wives. Often, he was the last one at the pub at night, after the others had gone home to their families.

Jonathan had gone to work for Avi right out of college and while he valued the experience, truthfully, there just weren't enough hours in the day to get the work done. This was especially true with their first company, which had been bootstrapped with a capital B and had nearly gone all to pot before they sold it. He just hadn't had time to develop a social life. Work always came first and there wasn't much time for anything else. Even now that this Company was well funded and the bootstrapping days were over, it still *was* his life.

He had tried the online dating services, but he couldn't imagine having dinner with, let alone sitting across the table for the rest of his life at breakfast, with the women he met. So, for Jonathan, it all came down to that it was just easier to be single and settle for being a workaholic and a football fanatic.

Jonathan went to the break room and got a bottle of water and grabbed a protein bar. Dinner. He decided to catch up on his email before going home. Front and center in the inbox was a reminder about an online radio broadcast that was one of his subscriptions. He had to look twice at the message, as he could have sworn that it had flashed when he sat down. He must really be tired.

He had been a subscriber to this channel on BlogTalkRadio since 2009 when it was launched, but he never seemed to have the time to listen to the shows. Tonight, he would take the time.

Tonight's interview was with Bob Burg, the co-author of *The Go-Giver*. Recently, Jonathan caught the tail end of an interview with Bob on TheBlaze TV, and was interested in hearing more about the Laws of Stratospheric Success that Burg had talked about on the show. *I could definitely use a taste of something stratospheric in my life right now.*

The funny thing was that this interview had apparently taken in place in the early days of the show in 2009. He briefly wondered why this particular interview would pop up now. When the intro music started to play, he actually got goose bumps.

The song was Nicole Nordeman's, "Legacy." Just today in the strategy session, Jonathan had wondered whether he would leave a legacy for the company in his new role or whether he should just give up and find another position in operations somewhere else. At the same time he pondered that option, he couldn't imagine leaving Avi. Yet the trend line on the monthly sales dashboard in front of him made him think that the possibility of leaving was getting more and more likely if the investment firm had anything to say about it.

Then FLASH! The first thing that he saw on the screen was the dramatic message, "Do you want to supercharge your sales efforts?" He heard himself saying, "YES!" Not only did he say it *aloud*, he was pretty sure that he said it really loud! Did anyone hear him? They might think he had lost his marbles. He thought, *Nice one! I wonder if anyone is still in the office?* Due to the hour, he strongly suspected that he was alone. The only lights on were the hall lights.

Another graphic on the screen showed that Bob Burg was also the author of a book called *Endless Referrals. Lord knows that I could use some new referrals right about now.*

He was a bit stumped at the title of Bob's book that would be discussed in the interview, *The Go-Giver. I've always heard that to be good in sales, one had to be a go-getter, yet here he is talking about giving.* Just as he had that thought, the interviewer asked the same exact question. And the bottom line is that it seems that we need to be both.

Bob Burg explained, "We want people to be both go-getters: people of action, and go-givers: people who are focused on providing value to others. What we don't want is for people to be go-takers: focused only on themselves. Not only is that not a good way to operate, it's also the least profitable."

That entire shift in focus thing that Bob seemed to stress, is what really stuck out in the interview.

Burg said, "The key is to move from an 'I-focus' or 'me-focus' to an 'other-focus.'" To always be looking for ways to bring value to the other party. After all, no one buys from you because you have a quota to meet or because you *really* need the money. They buy from you because they believe there's more value to them in doing business with you than in not doing business with you. And, you only get to that point by being intensely, totally and laser-focused on them and their issues."

He then emphasized the philosophy of he and his coauthor, John David Mann by saying that, "Money is simply an echo of value. It's the thunder to value's lightning."

Brilliant! I love that. Tampa was the lightning capital of the world and in fact the Hockey team bore that exact name. Perhaps those two things would remind him to focus on providing value. It made total sense to Jonathan that a shift in orientation to giving would be a more profitable way to operate. He smiled at that. He knew that whatever he did, he had to bring in more profitable business.

But it was the story of Joe, the main character, who learned about providing value to his customers that really got his attention. Joe wasn't making his quota for the quarter, a pressure that Jonathan now understood firsthand. Burg continued to talk about the Law of Value, leading with the statement that, "Your true worth is determined by how much more you give in value than you take in payment." Jonathan was pretty sure that Bob was not talking about the kind of discounting that Tim practiced just to try to get people to buy from him. Just as he said that to himself, the interviewer confirmed his thoughts when asking, "You're not a big believer in discounting your prices, are you Bob?"

Burg replied, "When you sell on low price, you're a commodity. When you sell on value, you're a resource. When you're positioned as a resource, a trusted resource, your customers are more loyal to you, they stay with you longer, and they are much more likely to refer you to others. So, learn how to understand and effectively communicate the value of your products or services. And remember, value is always in the eyes of the beholder. And that's your customer."

Burg was on to something. Something big.

As he continued to listen to the interview, it was pretty clear that the Law of Value was not about pricing, it was an attitude of really caring about your clients, and not just for this sale, but every sales and service interaction over the long term. Caring about the customer came second nature to Jonathan, but he had never thought about caring having anything to do with sales. Jonathan stopped the interview and bookmarked the show. He promptly went to Amazon to order the Kindle version of the book. He decided that in order to really grasp the Laws of Stratospheric Success, he should actually read the book before finishing the interview. He grabbed his tablet, ordered the book and packed the device in his briefcase, leaving his laptop behind for the first time in months.

Tonight, he would start reading *The Go-Giver* and then see what tomorrow would bring. For once, he was actually glad for the solitude that he would find in his apartment tonight. Jonathan was looking forward to tomorrow, also a first since the dreaded job swap.

Chapter 5

Defying Gravity

Tim hung around the meeting room after the final day of the three-day strategic planning session, hoping to talk to Amanda. She was the partner from the Firm that was responsible for the results of the Company. She was also the one that had the brilliant idea to swap the roles between he and Jonathan. He, of course, used the term brilliant loosely. The only bright spot was that Jake had ensured that the swap came with a promotion. Yes, the Senior Vice President title took away a little of the sting of the new role—but only a little.

The additional money that he was able to negotiate actually helped a lot and would begin to make a dent in his substantial credit card debt, but now he was concerned about the fact that in his new role, he wouldn't earn commissions like he did in his past role. He didn't like having to depend on the entire team to reach profitability before he was eligible for a bonus. He was used to being in control of his own destiny, so for that reason he wanted to appeal to Amanda to reconsider the now infamous swap.

Amanda was deep in conversation with Avi, and with the deep scowl that he saw on her face, it didn't look like it would be over anytime soon. He had been hoping that he could make Amanda see that putting him in this role was as ridiculous as trying to defy gravity, but with her dark mood, he nixed that idea. Tim packed up his stuff and headed back to his office, as he needed to get his laptop to work on the call center schedule tonight.

Customer Service was just not his gig and he found Operations utterly boring. The only bright spot was the implementation planning meeting, as it was very similar to the process he had taught to his team in outlining customer requirements. This was just taking it one step farther.

When Jake had told him about the swap, Tim had actually said to him, "You are kidding, right?" When Jake flatly said, "No. I'm not." Tim knew that he had to try talking to Amanda instead, as he was certain that it was her idea.

Secretly, he was actually glad that she hadn't been available. In his heart-of-hearts, he knew that talking to her would not likely have the desired effect. He was nearly twenty years younger than her and he wasn't certain that she even understood his generation. He was afraid that she would see him as a whiner, and that was definitely not the impression that he wanted to leave with her.

© marketoonist.com

I wish I could have the opportunity to get to know her one-on-one, but that just didn't seem to be in the cards. *She only seems to have time for Avi and of course her pet, Catherine.*

When Tim took over Customer Service and Operations, he had told his staff that he was open to new ideas.

Today he got a cartoon from the *Marketoonist* in his email that caused him to wonder if anyone took him seriously. He had heard Catherine talking about Tom Fishburne a few days ago. That spurred the thought, *I don't think she likes me. I think she is just jealous of my new title. I wonder if she the one who signed me up for the Marketoonist mailing list? Or perhaps someone from my team sent it to me anonymously, trying to make a point. I'm not sure which is worse.*

Tim struggled to reconcile his depression over the job swap. Deep down, he knew he was a winner. When he was a young boy his mom told him that he could excel at anything that he wanted. She said it so often that it eventually became baked into his DNA. Throughout middle school and high school, he was always the outgoing athlete, popular with kids of all ages and loved by his teachers. In the senior yearbook, he was voted most likely to succeed. He modeled throughout college, so he was more than just confident about his looks, and his diligent workout routine ensured that even at twenty-nine, he still had the physique of a high school athlete. Still, even though his mom's words continued to echo in his brain, Tim thought, *so I'm not enthusiastic about excelling in this particular role. Is that so bad to admit?*

Even as he asked himself the silent question, he knew the answer. *I have to at least try. Truly, I love the company and want it to succeed.*

The last few years had been hard, watching the profits dwindle and seeing Avi being forced to make the tough decision to sell a large piece of the company, which had been his baby. As Tim pondered his time there, he knew that his years with the company had been the best of his career. He had been the number one sales person two years in a row when Avi had promoted him directly into the VP role. Now, he was an SVP. That first promotion was just a year before the Firm had come into the picture. He was the youngest officer in the company and in the Firm's portfolio of businesses. *Truly it didn't get better than this.*

But the pressure was still on. Over the past year, there was a substantial drop in profits. It was the culmination of a number of things. Everything around them was accelerating and the products were just not keeping up with the marketplace and the competition. In his previous role in sales, the only way that they could compete was to discount the products. While he instinctively knew that wasn't the right tack to take, they just couldn't put sales on hold while the core products were retooled.

If you ask me, Catherine just isn't up to the challenge of running Marketing and Product Management. Like Jonathan, Tim knew she had been with Avi a long time, even in his previous venture, but he was certain that there was someone better for that role. Even though there was a big age gap between them, he found himself wondering if there had been a "thing" between Catherine and Avi.

Since Catherine had been put in the VP role, she never asked what he thought about the product line. There was no trust and definitely no collaboration. Each time she came up with what she thought was a new idea in the meeting yesterday, Tim reminded her of why those things hadn't worked in the past. He would have thought it was obvious to her. Then, in the meeting yesterday, she had offered, "Tim, I would be happy to walk your team through the features in the new release." He had a quick retort and sharply said, "I already took them through the new release last week. Didn't you pay attention to my update?"

He had felt satisfaction when he said it, but now he wondered if that was necessary. In the back of his mind, he heard his mom say, "If you can't say something nice Timmy, don't say anything at all." And then he immediately felt guilty for thinking that there was something more than a professional relationship between Catherine and Avi. His mom always put people and relationships first and encouraged Tim to think the best of people and give them the benefit of the doubt. She had done her best to drill that into him as a teen. *Clearly that one hadn't sunk in quite as deeply as her other life lessons.*

He certainly wasn't building up the kind of relationship that he had hoped he would have with Catherine and he knew that now more than ever, they had to work together to be successful. Clearly she had been in the business world much longer than he had, as he had heard stories about her being pregnant when she first met Avi. With the age of her oldest, that would bring her close to forty with nearly twenty years of experience under her belt. He remembered that Catherine was one of three children and between her and her siblings, they now had six kids. He envied her that. Tim was an only child, as was his wife, and although they had been married for five years, they didn't have kids yet.

■ ■ Dallas | 1987-2012 | Tim ■ ■

Tim grew up in the affluent Highland Park area of Dallas, Texas, and had spent a year tooling around Europe before starting college. Then he had done his Master's Degree in Business at Duke University, in North Carolina, where his dad had gotten his law degree. He had two sets of grandparents that were still alive and lived in Chapel Hill, which was within an hour of Durham. They were both from old money and lived in grand estate homes in the prestigious Governors Club area. When he went to stay with one of them on the weekends, he always got a home cooked meal or two, and his laundry magically was completed before he had to head back to school on Sunday evening. Both sets of grandparents loved having Tim close, and his parents were glad that he could check in on them frequently.

After graduation, with generous gifts from his grandparents, Tim had taken one more year off traveling around the world before he started work. *I was fortunate that my family had the resources to allow me my extended education.*

Tim's dad was a very successful attorney and his mom was a flight attendant for a major airline. While she didn't need to work, she loved the freedom that it gave her to fly to Paris for the weekend, just because she could! The cost to travel on his mom's flight benefits was a little like spending Monopoly money, so he took full advantage of the year off.

One of the smartest things that he did that year was to study Spanish in Costa Rica for a month before doing his stint in Central America and Mexico. The school had been a coffee farm that had been converted to a school. It was in the mountains outside of San Jose. He lived with a family that only spoke Spanish to him, even though they all understood and spoke perfect English. That immersion style of learning was the best for him. Now, in Florida, he found that speaking and understanding Spanish was a real asset. Tim also traveled to Australia and New Zealand, spent some time with friends from school in Bangalore, India and visited South Africa where he got to go on a safari, which had been a dream since he was in grade school.

He had watched his parents put their dreams on hold as he was growing up. His dad's law practice was very demanding and of course, and his mom was gone a lot with her job. After she had retired and his dad sold the firm to his partners, just three years later at the age of sixty-eight, his mom had a debilitating stroke and was now in a wheelchair. Tim's dad also suffered from congestive heart failure and now sported a pacemaker and a defibrillator. Tim vowed that he wasn't going to let that happen to him. He worked out religiously.

He had become a vegetarian about five years ago when he met and married Liz and had recently become gluten-free. His wife was a nutritionist and she was helping him battle the genetic predisposition to cardiac problems in his family through diet and exercise, plus what seemed like a ton of supplements.

They had met and had gotten married just two months after their first date. They met at a party at a hotel in North Dallas thrown by the singles dating company that they had both joined. He spotted Liz right as she walked into the party. She came in the door, paused just slightly scanning the room and then walked down the wide stairway at the entrance as if in slow motion, Tim was captivated. He recalled the lyrics from *Bad Things*, the theme from his favorite series, *True Blood*. It began, "When you came in, the air went out." The words were so true. He could barely breathe.

He decided there and then that he was going to make sure that they met. In her brief scan of the room, she had spotted Dru, the girl who was his account manager at the dating service. He took that as a sign and as casually as he could, he joined the two of them. After Dru hugged him, he introduced himself to the petite blonde and offered to buy them both a drink. A few minutes later, Dru drifted off to talk to some other members, leaving Tim and Liz there alone.

It was a tad awkward at first and he was a little taken aback as she kept looking at her watch. But when he asked her if he was keeping her from something Liz shared that she was going to Cancun in the morning and she needed to go home to pack. Tim was relieved, as he thought she was just bored with him, and then was thrilled when Liz had asked innocently if he wanted to go to Cancun with them. She said that she was going with a group of dear friends from California, where she had grown up and that there was plenty of room for him to join them. Liz and her friends had the use of a timeshare in Cancun for the week with two separate units, with one designated for the girls of course. With his mom's flight benefits, getting on a plane at the last minute was no problem at all. For a minute, he questioned being so impulsive with someone that he had just met, but he figured that if it was truly awful, he could just fly back home. Suffice it to say that it was anything but awful!

Tim and Liz were inseparable when they returned from Cancun. They had so much in common and it seemed as if they were always laughing. She was just as active as he was and they both loved vacationing at the beach. After two months, Tim wanted for them to move in together, but Liz convinced him instead to get married by a Justice of the Peace in Grapevine, Texas, near her office. With his flight benefits, they could easily fly to California to meet her parents. She was a little worried about telling them that they were already married. To make that announcement a little easier, they planned on having a big wedding four months later, so that they could celebrate publicly with friends and family and her mom would be able to be involved in every detail of her only daughter's wedding.

The ceremony was held in November of 2011 at the Methodist Church in Hurst, which had beautiful stained glass windows. Since she attended the wedding of a friend there a few years ago, Liz had dreamed of getting married there, with the sun streaming in through the beautiful windows. She forgot one important fact though, that a wedding at five in the afternoon in November would actually occur at dusk, and the beauty of the windows would be lost. Tim was such a stickler for detail, he couldn't believe that he didn't notice that fact either! It could have been that he was preoccupied. Tim had a new job and right after their honeymoon, he would be going to Tampa for training.

Three weeks before their wedding, the alumni office at Duke called him and told him about the job opportunity with Avi. The head of the placement office had called and said, "Tim, you will love Avi, the founder and CEO. This is his second startup. I went to MIT with him and we have kept in touch. When I heard about this job, it had your name written all over it. It may look like an entry level sales job, but you have to trust me, this company is going places. I wouldn't be surprised if within five years they are sold or go public."

It did sound like a perfect opportunity for him, and now that he was married, it was definitely time to settle down. So, he took the sales job. His commissions were great, so he and Liz traveled quite a bit. Liz decided to take some online classes to become certified as a life coach, as a natural extension of her experience as a nutritionist.

When Tim was promoted to head the sales department in early 2012, he and Liz moved to the Tampa area and bought a house on a marina, just thirty minutes from Clearwater Beach. It was the perfect time and place for her to launch her new life coaching business. Tim still ran a mile every morning before work and played tennis most weekends with Liz. They were fortunate to live in a gated community with courts right there. If he wasn't traveling, he sometimes played tennis at night after dinner with their neighbor, since most of Liz's coaching calls took place in the evenings. Since some of their neighbors owned boats, on many weekends, they also enjoyed time on the water.

Tim's goal was to get a boat of their own, so that they wouldn't have to rely on those invitations, but now, with the new job and without his fat commission checks, that was going to have to wait until he could be eligible for the executive bonus program and perhaps even earned equity in the company. Liz still hadn't yet become pregnant, but now that he wouldn't be traveling as much, perhaps they could get serious about starting a family. Other than the job swap and the stress of his new role, Tim lived a charmed life. He was grateful.

■ ■ Tampa | Present Day | Tim ■ ■

When Tim arrived in his office after the offsite meeting, he heard someone shout, "Yes!" somewhere down the hall. While he found that odd, he didn't really give it much thought. He just grabbed his laptop and headed to his car, since he was late already. As if on cue, his phone rang and it was his wife Liz. He felt guilty that waiting to talk to Amanda had caused him to leave later than normal and he hadn't thought to call home.

Liz's voice sounded different. She was excited and talking fast about someone named Rebel something or other. He had to ask her to slow down.

Liz said, "Today Helene invited me to join a women's network, known as the Executive Girlfriends' Group. She then sent me a link to their iTunes channel." Helene was her best friend. "Helene said that they were giving me three months free and there are tons of shows available online about leadership, growth, innovation, entrepreneurialism and giving. I thought maybe we could listen to some of them together."

Liz shared that today she had listened to one that she had really liked and since she knew that he had a fifty-minute drive home, she thought he might want to listen to it. To himself he was saying, *Yeah, yeah*, but didn't want to dampen her enthusiasm, so he just said, "Great Liz, send me the link and I'll listen on the way home."

When he got settled in the car, he heard the telltale beep from her text and what he saw next took his breath away. The author was Rebel Brown and the book was *Defy Gravity*. *I just used that phrase earlier to describe my struggle with the swap!* He shivered involuntarily. He knew that he had to listen to the show, even though it was geared toward executive women. He would keep an open mind as it seemed like he was somehow meant to listen to the show.

Rebel sucked him in right away with her statement about the status quo that, "The way we've always done it is the reason for the mess that we are in." As the youngest member of the executive team, he frequently challenged the way things had always been done, particularly from the older executives that were stuck in their ways. As he thought back to the offsite, he mused, *I know that it is crazy to say so, but it really is our best-selling product that is dragging the company down.*

Then he almost had to pull the car over when he heard Rebel say, "Everything around us is accelerating." *Didn't I just say that an hour ago too? Who is this Rebel? And why had Liz chosen today to join the women's group and listen to this particular program?* In fact, in the intro he heard the Interviewer say that someone else had been scheduled and Rebel was a last-minute substitution. *Freaky.*

The next thing out of Rebel's mouth did make him pull over. He couldn't believe his ears. She said that quite often what was dragging companies down were their best sellers and that, "Changing and evolving solutions were needed to respond to the needs of the clients." She then urged the listeners to think about the way that you are selling, packaging, delivering and servicing the client. Rebel continued by saying that the only way to get it right was to go to the "keepers of the truth."

In the split second before she continued speaking, he wondered if it was the front line—his team—that were the keepers of the truth. *I like the sound of that,* he thought.

The truth was that it made him feel important. But no, Rebel said that you had to listen to the customer. Not just our favorite customers, but also the customers that left you, those that bought from someone else and those that are mad at you. He had plenty of those and their names and faces immediately invaded his thoughts.

The last thing that he heard before he eased the car carefully back on the road was that you can't just go after the big client, giving the product away, hoping that you make it up in volume. She called that the "bright lights, big city" approach to growth.

Rebel must have been a fly on the wall in the meeting where Amanda announced the fateful swap, where he was telling her about the big client that he was about to snag, just as she told him to turn all of his files over to Jonathan. Suddenly, everything was clear to him and he knew what he had to do.

I have to step into my role with a new passion, as the Keeper of the Truth. I have just the way to tap into that truth.

As the interviewer thanked Rebel and repeated the name of the book, he made a mental note to order the book. He wanted to hear the rest of what this Rebel had to say. He loved her style of delivery. It wasn't academic at all. And he was a bit of a rebel himself.

He couldn't wait to discuss it all with Catherine and Jonathan on Monday. He sheepishly hoped Catherine would forgive him for his abrasive approach in the meeting, knowing instinctively that thought would make his mom proud. He made a mental note to call his mom this weekend.

Chapter 6

I'd Rather Be in Charge

■ ■ Tampa-New York | Present Day | ■ ■
Amanda, Private Equity Partner

As the three-day strategy session came to a close, Amanda was tired, and she was disappointed, and even somewhat embarrassed. She had been charged with the responsibility of this turn around and she had high hopes for the Company. She had experienced many sleepless nights since taking this latest role, and last night was no different. In addition to the stress of work, Amanda suffered from sleep apnea. She had to travel with a C-PAP machine, and the mask she had to wear often woke her up several times a night.

Avi, the CEO, was very intelligent and very talented. From the first time that they met nearly two years ago, she had loved his entrepreneurial energy and his intellectual curiosity. He had built and sold a tech services company prior to this one, and working together, she believed they could turn this one around. Today's strategy session was an important step in that process.

Amanda had selected the facilitator for the session based on a recommendation of one of her peers at her firm, but it was an unmitigated disaster. It seemed to her that the self-absorbed facilitator was pandering to her the whole time, more focused on how he could ingratiate himself with her firm to score additional gigs, than truly helping the Company achieve its goals with the session. And it seemed like he took some of the exercises off the Internet, without any tailoring whatsoever to his client.

Amanda had become a named partner in the Firm just six months before the investment in the Company and this was her first solo turn-around gig. She had spent the years since business school in a variety of roles, first with Ogilvy & Mather Worldwide, and then a stint in Mergers & Acquisitions with Procter and Gamble before being recruited as a junior partner in the Firm. She was the first woman and the first female to be named partner. It had taken her nearly twenty years, but she had made it. Her name was on the wall of their firm at their office on 9 West 57th Street in New York. Her office overlooked Central Park. She knew that her parents would be proud of her if they were still alive.

She had lost both of her parents in the same year, first her mom with a debilitating stroke, after six years in a wheelchair from her first stroke. Then nine months later, her dad died in his sleep, after years of heart problems. Both were just seventy-five years old.

Amanda was working hard on getting fit from the inside out. She was in her late fifties and had two teenagers, a boy and a girl. She wanted to make sure that she lived way beyond seventy-five, and wanted to be healthy and active so that she could enjoy seeing her kids get married and have children of their own. Yet, it was tough to focus on her health, when her job required fourteen to sixteen hour days and a lot of traveling. That made it tough to eat right, and after a long day, a glass of wine or single malt scotch always sounded so very good. One glass often morphed into two and sometimes three. And when her C-PAP machine woke her up, there was that lingering headache. She had to cut back.

Her marriage was about to become a casualty of the Firm. Her husband, Stephen, had started out being understanding of the demands of her job, but with each promotion, and the more she worked late, or had to entertain or travel on business, his calm, easygoing demeanor slowly dissolved into smoldering, then explosive anger.

When growing up, she had never had to deal with anger, as her dad was very quiet and her mom was always happy, or at least she seemed so. Her dad was a pastor and her mom was a music teacher, both very even tempered. Her mom had stayed active in music even after she stopped teaching. Just weeks before her stroke, her mom had a part in the production of *Joseph's Technicolor Dream Coat* at church.

No one ever screamed or yelled in her home, so she didn't have the training to deal with Stephen's frequent mood swings and his curse-laden outbursts. Stephen didn't have a good model for a father or husband. His dad was an alcoholic, like his father before him. He had a very volatile personality, alternating from the passive, quiet intellectual, to bursts of anger. His mom had just been the subservient peacekeeper in the house. That wasn't how Amanda saw this playing out for herself.

Just a month ago, they decided to separate. Stephen wasn't willing to consider counseling. He had moved in with his sister and her husband, who lived in the city. They knew that it would be tough on the kids, but the volatility of their relationship over the past eighteen months had been even harder on them. Stephen called this a cooling off period, but Amanda feared that it would become permanent. Amanda thought she would lose weight after they separated, but she had actually gained another twenty pounds.

■ ■ ■ ■

During the last break of the day as the offsite session was ending, Amanda flashed back to yesterday's review of the product line. Catherine had tried to put forward some new ideas. Amanda had been coaching her since taking over her role on the board, as Catherine was the only woman on the executive team.

At first, she was a little intimidated by Catherine, who was the antithesis of Amanda physically. Catherine was petite, fit and even training to climb Mount Kilimanjaro. Even though she was confident and secure in every other area of her life, or had been before her separation, Amanda was very self-conscious about her weight. It had been a lifelong struggle for her. Catherine wore fashionable, colorful clothes and Amanda perpetually wore black. Last week during their regular session, Catherine gave Amanda an insight into her reasons for doing the climb.

"A few months ago, I listened to a radio show for a women's network that I belong to and the person interviewed had written a book called, *Up: Pursuing Significance in Leadership and Life.* Joan O'Sullivan had climbed Mount Kilimanjaro. She said, *up is the direction of humanity's finest pursuit, and significance is the hope of every soul on this planet.* Right there and then, I decided that I was going to do it."

Amanda told her, "I so admire your discipline, Catherine. I know that you will find what you are looking for. Hey, could you send me an invitation to the woman's group? Now that my husband has moved into the city, I am going to have some extra time on my hands and it would be good to do some networking outside my industry." She had confided in Catherine about her separation a few weeks earlier, even though she made a practice of keeping her private life private. Amanda made a mental note to order the book Catherine told her about.

Perhaps I can find my own brand of significance, even though I have no intention of climbing a mountain to find it. That would be the day!

Amanda knew from her work in mergers and acquisitions over the past twenty years that companies with women on their executive teams and boards are measurably more profitable than their male dominated peers. In fact, they are 66% more likely to outperform those without female board members when it comes to seeing a return on invested capital. That was important to her firm, so she was on the lookout for female board members for the company.

At breakfast this morning with Avi, she encouraged him to recommend a new outside board member at the upcoming board meeting and she shared the stats with him, hoping that he could recommend a woman for the open board position. Avi needed to get refocused. He seemed to have lost his entrepreneurial spirit since the takeover, and he no longer talked about the seeds of innovation. She thought, *it was a shame really, as that passion had been one of his most attractive traits.*

IF IT WERE REALLY A GOOD IDEA,
SOMEONE WOULD ALREADY BE DOING IT,
AND WE WOULD FOLLOW LATE TO MARKET
WITH AN UNDIFFERENTIATED KNOCK OFF

© marketoonist.com

At the product line review yesterday when he knocked down any idea that Catherine shared, Amanda had felt like she was in the cartoon that Catherine had shared with her just last week.

The product line was indeed undifferentiated and they just weren't gaining any traction against their competitors.

She had thought that swapping Jonathan and Tim's roles would inject some fresh thinking and energy into both Sales and Customer Service, but she sensed that both men were struggling in their new roles. That was especially true of Jonathan who had the additional sting of Tim's promotion. When she heard about the plan, Amanda had asked Jake "Do you really think that this is the right time for the promotion?" Jake had reminded her that, "Tim invested in himself by getting his MBA and we owe it to him to recognize it."

Amanda knew that the Firm highly valued graduate degrees and it didn't escape her that Tim's MBA was from Jake's alma mater. She had battled the good 'ole boy network for long enough not to notice. While she had her MBA (and in fact two Master's), she held the unpopular view that those that took the entrepreneurial path had learned the same basic lessons, but with a practical spin.

Where she had spent significant money to get her degrees, they paid with sweat equity and usually a fair amount of blood, sweat and tears.

The first time she met with Catherine she had to laugh when she was preparing for the meeting. Catherine's bio on LinkedIn said that she earned her graduate degree from the School of Hard Knocks. When she asked her about it, Catherine said, "Just today my seventeen-year-old daughter asked me where the school was located!" They both laughed heartily when Catherine recounted her response "It is everywhere!"

Catherine was as smart as a whip and Amanda suspected that she could run circles around Tim if she were in charge of Customer Service and Operations. In fact, yesterday when Jake cornered Tim about the call center stats, Catherine had quietly handed Jake the call center report. She could have crushed him verbally, but she didn't. Once again Amanda admired her discipline and self-control. *Perhaps some of that would rub off on Tim. Or not.*

After her last session with Catherine, Amanda had vowed to get to know the rest of the team better, to understand what made them tick and what motivated them. It wasn't always the obvious. And she knew that becoming better as a team begins with getting to know each other, perhaps even as friends.

The format of the offsite meeting didn't allow for the kind of interaction with the executive team that she had hoped. Last night at dinner, she was cornered at her end of the table by the facilitator who dominated the conversation all night. *Ugh.*

She well understood that in order to succeed with the turn around, she had to first transform from being the unwelcome outsider to truly being seen as a part of the team. Then they could transform the Company together. She recalled a line from the *Rhythm of Life* by Matthew Kelly. "The people we surround ourselves with either raise or lower our standards. They either become the best version of ourselves or encourage us to become lesser versions of ourselves. We become like our friends. No man becomes great on his own. No woman becomes great on her own. The people around them help to make them great. We all need people in our lives who raise our standards, remind us of our essential purpose and challenge us to become the best version of ourselves."

She felt like she and Avi were making some strides and he really did raise her standards and bring out the best in her, but she hadn't really connected with Tim or Jonathan yet. She sensed that they were actually angry with her about the swap, believing that it was her idea. As the senior partner, she would take full responsibility, even though it had been Jake's idea.

Someone had recently shared with her that Tim's mother had experienced a stroke at the same age as her mother, so she made a mental note to ask how she was doing the next time she they were together. *Perhaps reaching out to him will begin to bridge the two generations between us.*

Jonathan hadn't looked her in the eyes at all over the past three days, yet she had been pleased with his contribution during the brainstorming session. His love for the company shined clearly when he spoke. *He has promise in his new role. If he digs deeply enough, he will see it himself,* she speculated. *And yes, some of the members of his sales team were mavericks, but if you fire all the mavericks, then everyone left is so agreeable that nothing moves forward.* She remembered hearing that phrase at a session with her former company, Ogilvy, which had been P&G's ad agency. It stuck with her.

She also promised herself that she would get to know Jake, the CFO, better. They had worked together on other projects, but never side by side like they were now.

The facilitator was trying to get everyone back in the room, so Amanda stopped her musing and took her chair. As she was waiting for the final session to start, she looked at her iPad and saw a Facebook notification from the executive women's group that Catherine had told her about. She had recently joined as a part of her "re-invent Amanda" campaign.

Her counselor had encouraged her to invest some time in herself and perhaps even make some new friends outside of the Financial Services sector. Many of the members were a part of the travel industry, and the Firm had a number of investments in that sector, including the Company, which focused on technology for the hospitality and events industry. The group had just posted the audio interview with Charlotte Beers about a book she had written called *I'd Rather Be in Charge.* Amanda was excited and quickly bookmarked the email since it looked like the meeting was about to start.

Charlotte had been the CEO at Ogilvy and Mather during her tenure there. In her last year at the company, Charlotte had appeared on the cover of *Fortune*, their first issue to feature the most powerful women in America. Charlotte had gone on to be the Undersecretary of State under Colin Powell, someone that Amanda greatly admired.

It would be great to hear about what had transpired since they were both at Ogilvy.

■ ■ ■ ■

The last hour of the meeting was more of the "facilitator show" and her dismay was thinly veiled. She should have had the courage to toss out the facilitator after the first day and run the meeting herself. She knew that she was just accommodating his style, so as not to upset the applecart with her colleague at the Firm. This was not working to the Company's advantage. After the meeting, she quickly went over to Avi and talked about how they could get back on track after such a bad experience over the last three days.

"I want you to know Avi that I take full responsibility for the facilitator debacle. I should have had him spend time with the team before the workshop." Amanda spoke firmly and held her shoulders straight, but that belied how she was feeling inside. Amanda continued, "I have some ideas to bounce off of you on how to recover from this disaster. Do you have time next Monday? I think that we need to get the team refocused and show that we have a plan to move the Company forward."

Avi said, "I totally agree. And Amanda, I want you to know how appreciative I am of your honesty and willingness to admit the setback caused by the meeting. I had put a lot of hope in this session to move us forward and I am sure that the team shared that optimism." Although Amanda could have taken that in criticism, she instead made the choice to see it as common ground, propelling them closer to becoming a true team.

By the time they were finished, everyone had left the room. Amanda had noticed Tim hanging around after the meeting and was relieved that he had finally gone. She needed time to regroup before listening to his concerns about his new role.

She had taken some time out of her counseling session last week to talk to her therapist about Tim. Her counselor had given her some great advice on how to deal with him, but Amanda still needed a little more time before sitting down with him. *I want it to be on my terms. I don't want to feel cornered.*

Truth be known, these days she felt like a failure; and not just in her marriage. She pondered everything that had happened over the last few months and thought, *I want to be fierce and strong in my new role and to help the company dramatically change the name of the game.* But the debacle of the last three days and the dysfunction in her marriage robbed her of so much. She had really expected to see positive change by now on both fronts, with the company and her husband.

Amanda dropped her rental car off at the Tampa International Airport and braved the check-in line and security. She loved having the TSA Pre√ on her boarding pass and breezed through the security check point with her shoes and jacket intact. The Tampa airport was a pleasure to travel through, particularly compared to LaGuardia or JFK, or Miami, where her last investor client had been. It was recently voted the top large airport in the country by travelers. She could see why.

When settled into seat 2A on the non-stop to JFK, she was once again grateful that there was a material benefit to all the travel that she did. She had been Platinum on Delta for more than a decade. Of course, she had missed her kids growing up, but was grateful for their live-in nanny. The nanny was more like a sister to the kids than a household employee, and now that Amanda's husband was living in the city, she needed her more than ever.

As soon as the door on the plane closed, she put her headphones on and quickly turned to the channel for the interview with Charlotte Beers. She was happy that Delta has Wi-Fi on the plane because she had forgotten to download the show ahead of time. Listening to the interview would make the flight home go much faster.

Amanda was looking forward to the weekend. Her best friend was coming for dinner tomorrow night and the kids would be with Stephen. It had been too long since they had spent time together. She had gone through a painful divorce recently and Amanda vowed to herself that they wouldn't spend the whole night talking about marriage woes. *No, this weekend was a time to focus on the future.*

The flight attendant brought her a glass of chardonnay and some warmed mixed nuts and she clicked the arrow on her iPad and eagerly started on the show. Hearing Charlotte's voice brought back warm memories. She didn't actually know her on a personal level, but had been in many company meetings at Ogilvy and Mather where Charlotte would share her vision, as well as the firm's results. Amanda had loved working for an exceptionally smart woman.

Charlotte started talking about one of her leadership roles where she was brought in as a "talented change agent, surrounded by extremely remarkable people."

Amanda wondered whether anyone would ever describe her in that way.

Am I actually a change agent? Does anyone see my talent? Sometimes I feel like a babysitter versus being in charge of a turnaround for the Firm.

Although the travel industry was fun, this investment project just wasn't high profile enough for them and she suspected that she got it because none of her male counterparts wanted it. As she was musing on her own situation, she heard Charlotte talk about her role as Under Secretary of State, working primarily in Afghanistan and Iraq, where she clearly operated in a man's world. But she didn't seem to be daunted by it. In fact, Charlotte said that, "The problem isn't with men, it is how we see ourselves as women."

That was a wakeup call for Amanda. Many times over the last twenty years, she attended client meetings where she was the only woman at the table. Rather than see what a gift that was, she would feel intimidated by the men with all of their Ivy League degrees and mentions of their country club lifestyles.

She remembered one merger back in 2001 where she was sitting with a female executive from the acquiring firm around the enormous conference table that easily sat sixty people. They were the only women at the table, although there were several in supporting roles sitting in the row of chairs by the wall. The woman had whispered to her during the meeting that she didn't even have a degree, and here she was surrounded by all of these "suits." They had laughed about it and later Amanda had told her how proud she was that she had been willing to make that admission to her. They were still very close friends today. In fact, when Stephen left, Flo had been the first one that she called.

Amanda was definitely smart enough to have gone to an Ivy League school, but her immigrant parents simply didn't have the money and she didn't want to graduate with massive debt. Since her parents grew up in western Poland, Amanda had chosen the University of Warsaw in Poland for her undergraduate degree. Some called her crazy, as Poland was still under Communist rule. But with dual citizenship, she was able to enter the country on her Polish passport and she was fluent in Polish. It was certainly not as prestigious as the Ivy League schools, but it did boast of five Nobel laureates. Best of all, it was unbelievably affordable and she was able to complete the entire program in five years, instead of six.

Amanda loved the Polish people and the school had students from nearly every country in Europe, as well as around the globe. They also brought in many amazing speakers. One of Amanda's favorite speakers was in her last semester in the program. Kofi Annan, the former Minister of Tourism from Ghana (who would later become the Secretary General of the UN), was one of the speakers.

Amanda would never forget it, as it was on a Friday afternoon and the speaker began his talk with a hearty laugh, saying that today was his day! There is apparently a custom in Ghana to name your child after the day of the week on which he or she was born, and he and his twin sister were born on Friday. Annan means Friday in his language! She didn't know that day, but he would have a profound impact on her future. Annan had told the audience that day, "Follow your own inner compass...know who you are, what you stand for, where you want to go, and why you want to get there."

When she returned to the US, because of her degree and her exposure to so many cultures in Poland, Amanda was in high demand and was fortunate to have her pick of opportunities. She knew that she wanted to work in the tech field, so in the fall of 1978 before diving into her corporate career, she decided to take Annan's advice and follow her inner compass about what is next. Although it was expensive, she decided to get a student loan and attend the Sloan Fellows program at MIT. Annan was an alumnus of the program from 1972, and had spoken highly of his experience there. Although she already had her Master's degree in International Business, this would give her the prestigious MBA from Sloan to add to her credentials.

What she didn't know at the time was that she would go through the program with Stephen's best friend's father, Robert Kuhn, who was an expert on Chinese business strategy. Robert invited her to their home for Thanksgiving in November of 1978, she later learned, to introduce her to his son, hoping for some spark between them. Instead she fell for Aaron's friend Stephen. After the holiday meal, she and Stephen became inseparable and spent every holiday and summers together, as well as many weekends. They were married when she graduated from Sloan in 1980. She went on to join Ogilvy and Mather.

Then Amanda thought back on the early days of her marriage. When she and Stephen got married, they didn't have a country club membership. They lived in a beautiful, but simple mid-century house on the water in Stamford, Connecticut. It had been his parent's house. They had died tragically in a car accident when he was in college and left it to him.

Amanda had loved spending time together on the weekends as a family. During the week, Stephen traveled into the city for his job as a film editor, so they shared the ride on the train each day. That was before the tension set in and weekends were more about walking on eggshells than enjoying one another.

Amanda and her daughter had recently gone on a mission trip to southwestern Poland, very close to where her parents had met. Elise had decided to follow in her mother's footsteps, only she was going to study Psychology. She had decided to apply for the elite WISP (Warsaw International Studies in Psychology) program, which only accepted forty-four students each year. If she got in, she would be there for the two-hundred-year anniversary of the University in the fall. Amanda needed to mark that very special date down on her calendar. It would be a great bonding time with Elise, who had taken her parents separation very hard.

Just then, the interviewer jumped in and reminded the audience of the book title, and for the first time mentioned the sub-title, *Achieving Pride, Power and Joy at Work*. Based on where her thoughts had been, she knew that she was struggling on the pride and power part, but it was the last one that really grabbed her attention. *Joy. When was the last time that she used that term to describe her work? Uh, never?*

Then Charlotte shared that, "The work environment is cluttered with expectations about women." I chuckled when she said that they were expected to be "womanly" and she thought the term should be "leaderly." For some reason, that made Amanda laugh out loud. Then Charlotte challenged the listeners to "think about who you are at work, versus who you are at home and who you are in the relationships at work."

Relationships take time, Amanda thought. *And time is my most precious commodity. But it is an investment that I know that I have to make to turn this company around.* And with the pending sacrifice of her marriage, she knew that she had more to turn around than just the company.

Then Charlotte jolted her back by talking about being fierce and strong and to "find the stranger within" that had those traits. *Wow, it hadn't been more than three hours since she had chided herself for not dealing with the facilitator with exactly those two characteristics.* She knew that she had lost a bit of who she was as she dealt with her struggles with Stephen. Charlotte also talked about being "accommodating to our disadvantage," and she was reminded about not taking the steps on the first day to fire the facilitator. *Wow again.*

As the flight attendant refilled her glass and brought her dinner, she moved her iPad to the seatback pocket, but didn't turn it off. She couldn't stop now. She felt like she was somehow meant to listen to this very show—today, now.

Charlotte was now talking about stepping into a "leadership moment." She described that moment as the time when you "sweep everyone up into a direction that they haven't thought of." *She is talking about being a game changer,* Amanda thought. *That is what I really long to be. That is honestly what would give me joy.*

She could tell that the show was about to wrap up and she didn't want to miss anything, so she put down her fork and just listened. Charlotte's last point was that if you "wait until you have done all your homework before stepping out, you are just part of a good management team." Boy, Amanda sure knew that. Doing your homework thoroughly was the most basic responsibility of anyone in private equity. Charlotte continued to say, "But if you step out with absolutely no proof that what you say is true, that is true leadership. And persuading others is the very definition of leadership."

The interviewer ended by reading something from the end of the book that said for the reader (or in Amanda's case the listener), the book was not ending; instead, a new chapter in the reader's story is opening. Charlotte closed the interview by saying that she really had wanted to name the book, "I'd rather you be in charge," because she wanted to empower others and spur them to that kind of leadership. Then Amanda's thoughts turned again to her marriage, and she found herself wondering if last line was for her husband or for Avi, or maybe both of them. As the Interviewer signed off, Amanda could feel her new story begin to unfold.

She was beginning her new journey and she had a feeling that her meeting with Avi on Monday would take a very different turn than what she had originally planned. And she made the bold decision to ask her husband to join her in her counseling session next week and, handing the flight attendant the unfinished Chardonnay, she decided to also cut back on her drinking.

Once again she mused Kofi Annan's admonition. "Follow your own inner compass…know who you are, what you stand for, where you want to go, and why you want to get there."

For once, I have total clarity on all four points.

Chapter 7

He Who Dares, Wins

■ ■ Tampa | Present Day | Avi ■ ■

Avi was beyond exhausted. The strategy session had been an abject failure and even though Amanda took responsibility for the selection of the facilitator, he couldn't shake the feeling that he should have done something about it. *The guy had chutzpah, and not the good kind.*

It reminded him of when he had seen film *The Poseidon Adventure* in 1972, just after he had emigrated from Israel to the US. The entire second half of the movie was distressing to Avi. He wanted to walk out, particularly after the ship capsized, but he was afraid of what his date would say if he admitted his fear of drowning. Later on, he told her, "I really wanted to walk out when Shelley Winters was underwater!" She had responded, "I was feeling exactly the same thing Avi, but I was being brave because I thought you would think I was weak." *If only I had had the courage, then—and now—to act on my instincts.*

The facilitator of the strategy session had played it safe, not wanting to rock the boat. Funny metaphor really, considering the movie analogy. *If he had spent any time with me prior to the meeting, he would have known that this was not the time to be conservative. The Company needed change. Radical change.*

All eyes were on Avi. *And why not? I am the CEO after all*. Yet, anyone close to him had to know that he was no longer calling the shots. He had to tread lightly with the board members and in particular with Amanda. She had been brought in to turn this place around, and even though he was a decade older, he somehow felt inferior when he was around her. Which was funny, since the last time they were together she had told him that he brought out the best in her. He had wondered for an instant if she was coming on to him. He had heard rumors that she and her husband were having problems.

Perhaps his real problem was that Amanda had done so much better than he had with her Master's degree from MIT Sloan, or that she was able to land a plum job with Ogilvy and Mather right out of school. From Avi's perspective, her real advantage was her experience in attending an unorthodox international school. Or that Procter and Gamble had recruited her to work on mergers when she was still in her early thirties. Or that the Firm had recruited her just a few years later as a partner and now had brought her in to fix *his* company.

Just last week, in a private moment over a beer at Jonathan's favorite pub in Carrollwood, Avi said, "It just isn't right that someone younger, and not just younger, but a woman was brought in to turn the Company around." Avi was raised to respect women, but in his patriarchal culture, men were definitely the leaders. When he and Jonathan were together like this, they were not boss and employee, but dear old friends.

Truth be known, Amanda was only four years younger than Avi, but he continued on his diatribe, "And you know that as a partner in her firm, she gets to participate in the financial gains when they sell off pieces and parts of a company or when they take them public—all without the sleepless nights. It just doesn't seem fair."

Jonathan agreed. Although he was younger than Avi, he was still old school. "Besides, she has never been an entrepreneur. And I'm sure that she doesn't have a clue what it is like to pay MasterCard with an advance on your Visa card, or to borrow money from your 401k to cover payroll."

Avi laughed and slapped Jonathan on the back. "Brother, I'm glad those days are finally gone!" Jonathan raised his pint to Avi and said "Amen to that, mate!"

Avi knew that there were changes needed in every area within his company and despite what he had said to Jonathan about Amanda, he truly didn't begrudge the private equity team the rewards they would get when they successfully turned the Company around. He knew many other entrepreneurs that had resisted taking in investment capital and they were all struggling.

This was his big chance.

Perhaps, they would even take the Company public! He suspected that was the reason that they had brought in their CFO when they completed the transaction. Jake was smart, but he was all business. Avi hadn't really meshed with him at all. While he thought that he understood financial matters, around Jake he felt like an idiot.

Each time he sat with Jake, the new CFO was armed with the Dashboard, a tool that had the top line results and bottom line impact of what he called KPIs. Avi had to look up KPI (Key Performance Indicators) on Investopedia.com. That site helped him understand the many new terms that his PE investors used. The days were long gone when his gut feeling was the KPI for the business!

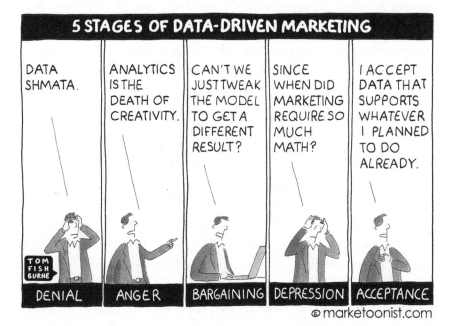

Jake was forever talking about data-driven marketing. Avi had to laugh, as Catherine had sent him one of her now infamous cartoons just yesterday, telling him that he seemed to already be in the third stage of data-driven marketing!

This afternoon's discussion with Jake at the last break focused on the sales results for the last quarter. Jake had not been smiling, and looking at the graphic had a similar impact on Avi. He felt himself regressing to the second stage portrayed on the cartoon—anger. He found himself almost quoting the character, saying, "Analytics is the death of creativity." But he decided to hold his tongue.

The Sales Department was the lifeblood of the Company. Although they didn't charge a huge amount for their main product, getting firms to use their product on a private label basis within their website was critical to the company's transactional, recurring revenue stream. Their core revenues came from the transactional use of their unique trip-planning tool. Once this product was adopted by their clients, they could literally make money while they slept. At least theoretically. That was one of the key attractions for the Firm to the product concept. Not only could it potentially change the game for an entire industry, effectively taking the old guard by surprise, but the revenues could also grow exponentially without corresponding growth in the support infrastructure. It was brilliant and it was Avi's brainchild.

A few weeks ago, Amanda had taken Tim, their star sales person, and shifted him to an SVP role in Customer Service. Avi still didn't understand her motivation there. When he asked her, she explained, "Tim may have been the top sales person for the private label product line, but he just isn't well rounded enough to lead the sales team to the next level. With his educational background, we think that he could bring some fresh insights to Catherine on the product front as well, once he understands the customers better." Avi couldn't argue with her logic. She continued, "Likewise, until Jonathan sees things from the other side of the fence, he won't be able to create a world-class service organization to support a broader product line. That is, if we decided to return him to that role."

A part of Avi knew that Amanda was right, but it was painful to watch the two men grapple with the job swap. He had thought about asking her to explain Tim's promotion, but decided against it, since she might see it as a further reflection of his admitted loyalty to Jonathan. Both men had confided in Avi, believing that the decision came from Amanda. It was all that he could do not to criticize the decision in his discussions with Tim and Jonathan, but he knew that he had to support his new business partners. Without the Firm, he literally wouldn't be in business today.

He had hated having to ask for help, but last spring, he knew that without an infusion of cash, his company had ninety days left, if that. Avi had already leveraged almost everything that he owned, and the bank had recently repossessed his prized 27-foot Regal cabin cruiser. His son loved to use it for fishing, so it was especially heartbreaking for Avi to let it go. Jonathan had been very supportive through this whole thing, even when he found out that his equity position in the company was being seriously crunched down as a result of the Firm's investment. But, if they were able to turn things around, it would all work out favorably for everyone, even Jonathan. Avi had to keep reminding himself that thirty percent of a five-hundred-million-dollar company was worth way more than one hundred percent of nothing.

Avi knew that he was extremely fortunate to have people like Jonathan and Catherine by his side. The two of them were not only there to help him with things that were not in his skillset or interest, but they had his back as well. You couldn't put a price on that kind of loyalty. Avi was passionate about his life as an entrepreneur and was hoping that once they got an executable strategy in place, that he could start doing the things that he loved again.

It was odd. This morning as he was shaving, he looked at himself in the mirror and it occurred to him that there was no joy in what he was doing right now. He thought, *joy is an odd term to use! It hasn't ever been a part of my vocabulary, certainly not about my work. Perhaps fun is a more accurate term.* Then he paused as he pondered that notion. *No, it doesn't go nearly deep enough.*

He turned his attention quickly away from himself to the task at hand. Before his meeting with Amanda on Monday, he wanted to have some concrete ideas on what to do next to get the company back on track and to move the needle significantly for the next quarter. In fact, he was going to be bold and say that he was going to start focusing on the long term again, as that was clearly the role of the CEO. And it was his personal sweet spot.

He often used the analogy of a lifeguard at the beach when he talked about his role as CEO. He was on the chair that sat high above the beach, looking out over the water for sharks or boats that had strayed too close to shore and keeping his eye out for storms on the horizon. The lifeguards who walked the beach were more like his leadership team, paying attention to the dangers that they could see from their vantage point. They kept small children from going into the water when their mothers' backs were turned and if someone did get out too deep, the lifeguards would swim out to get them. They needed each other and everyone worked hand-in-hand.

It was much like the leadership team within a company. Using that same analogy, the Firm was like the Coast Guard, radioing those on shore when there was danger they couldn't readily see or warning them of impending bad weather, not yet visible on the horizon. And funding the resources needed to keep the beach safe. He knew how very important it was for all of them to work together toward the same goals.

■ ■ ■ ■

Avi's wife, Sarah, was out of town on business. She worked for Hewlett-Packard doing project management for its enterprise systems, and this weekend, there was a big cutover for one of her key clients in Dallas. She was staying with her best friend Chris, who headed up sales for a manufacturing company. She and Chris had met on a project at Ericsson Wireless years ago. The women were a week apart in age and when they were together, they could finish one another's sentences. Chris' husband was also the same age as Avi. The two couples got along well and they were overdue to get together. He jotted a note down on his desk calendar to call John on Monday and make the arrangements.

The kids were spending the night at his in-laws, so for once, Avi didn't have to hurry home. He always felt unspoken pressure to be home early when Sarah was in town, as he remembered his promise to her the weekend in Boston that he proposed. No more being a workaholic.

He decided that he would just take the time tonight to get his thoughts together for his Monday meeting and stop to pick up takeout Thai food on his way home. He pulled the menu out of his top desk drawer and put it by his phone so that he would remember to place the order before he started his drive home.

Avi remembered getting an email from another colleague in the travel industry about a Tampa-based firm that had a unique integrated planning approach. Dave had told him that in just two-and-a-half days, the local company had a measurable, executable project plan to achieve their stated strategy and the Facilitator even provided the program manager to keep everyone on track. By the end of the first year, Dave's firm had accomplished over ninety percent of what they set out to do and they increased revenues over two hundred percent. *Wow.*

He took a quick break and got a coke to tide him over until he could enjoy his favorite, pad Thai, with curry puffs and cucumber salad as an appetizer. He didn't want to spoil his appetite, so he resisted the urge to grab a Snickers bar as well. As he walked back to his office, he saw that Jonathan's light was still on, but he walked the long way around. *I am not prepared to engage in a deep philosophical discussion around the swap tonight. I love Jonathan, but tonight I just don't have the energy.*

When he got back to his desk, his first task was to find the contact information for the woman from the integrated planning firm. As he looked for the email from his colleague with the firm's name, on the top of the search list was an email about a radio show that the firm's founder had done on leadership. That was a good sign. With hosting a radio show, it sounded like she made sure that she constantly exposed herself to fresh concepts. That intellectual curiosity was really important to him. She had an unusual first name that sounded familiar, but he couldn't place where he had met her. His memory just wasn't what it used to be. Then he saw the pictures of her board of directors and saw Sarah's best friend Chris was on her board. *That must be where I heard her name.*

The email that popped up was promoting an interview with the author of *Think Like Zuck*. The author's name was Ekaterina Walters. It struck him as funny that this email would pop up now, especially since the date on the show was March of 2013. While he suspected that the show was recorded, he thought it would be more current.

Avi had secretly admired what Zuckerberg created, even though he was young and as the book subtitle stated, *an improbably brilliant CEO*. Avi would love to be considered brilliant, improbably or otherwise!

When Facebook took off and truly changed how we communicate, network and share our lives, Avi had been a little jealous of Zuckerberg. Mark Zuckerberg had gone to school in Cambridge as well, at Harvard. Granted it was several decades later, but he felt an affinity with him nonetheless.

Since coming to the US in the early '70s to attend MIT, Avi had wanted nothing more than to be seen as a true game changer. His dream was to leave a legacy by redefining his industry with his ideas to apply technology to various problems that he observed with the old guard of the industry. His parents had heard about the school from close American friends who had moved from the states to Tel Aviv in 1967, just days after the Six-Day war. Avi had been in high school then and was a bit fearful about doing his upcoming compulsory military service with so much conflict going on around the globe.

Even though Cambridge, Massachusetts had been a hotbed of protests since the Vietnam War had begun, his parents agreed that MIT would provide Avi with the education he needed to achieve his dream. It was a plus that his friend Benjamin was going to be attending MIT as well. They had concluded that Avi was mature enough to find his way, even amidst the student rebellion against the war.

Since Avi didn't have the pressure to get home, he decided to click on the link and listen to at least the first part of the interview to see if he would glean anything worthwhile. He put his feet up on his desk and closed his eyes. What he heard next caused him to sit back up, eyes open, on full alert.

The author was an immigrant from Russia, from the same region as his grandparents. His grandmother had fled Russia when it became dangerous for Jews to live in her village. Her husband, a professor of philosophy, had been shipped off by the Gulag to a prison camp in Siberia, where he had succumbed to pneumonia the first winter. Heartbroken, his grandmother had moved with friends to Jerusalem in what is now known as Israel, bringing along his mother. She was fifteen at the time. She learned to sew from her mother and opened up a shop that did alterations, which is where she met father, who ran the inn down the road. The rest was history.

He snapped back to the present and Ekaterina's story. "My job is to redefine a key part of Intel's strategy as it relates to the emergence of social media," said the author.

Wow. Intel had a one hundred-sixty-billion-dollar market cap and they gave this young woman a blank canvas to work from, plus the funds to implement a new social media strategy? She called herself an intrapreneur, which he knew was the act of behaving like an entrepreneur while working within a large organization. He thought back to the group he had worked with in the '80s within AMR. *I hope that Ekaterina fared better than the woman I dealt with there.*

What Ekaterina was saying also gave him hope, as he had begun to believe that he would have to leave entrepreneurialism behind once he took in the private equity investment, but she reiterated that it was the entrepreneurial spirit that was key to success.

As she spoke about her role at Intel, he realized that like Ekaterina, he now had the resources and capabilities of the Firm at his disposal to launch new ideas, without having to bootstrap. That reminded him of why he sold a portion of the Company. *It wasn't just to get bailed out. It was to move the Company forward.* It was a liberating thought.

Just as he came to that realization, he heard the Interviewer say that Ekaterina had done a TED talk. The TED organization is a non-profit organization devoted to spreading ideas, in the form of short, powerful talks. Avi frequently listened to TED talks in his car on the way home and on the days that he picked up the kids, they enjoyed them as well. Another of his secret dreams was doing his own TED talk about planting the seeds of innovation. He wanted to share how the laws of nature simply did not allow seeds to be watered and not produce precisely what was planted.

Avi vowed to come back to the radio show interview later and decided to watch Ekaterina's talk on TED.com now. He quickly found it using their search tool. It was her personal story about being a first-generation Russian immigrant to the US. As he watched the talk, although decades apart in age, he realized that there were so many parallels in their lives. She too had a grandmother that had been a strong, brave role model. And Ekaterina had come to the United States to get her education.

She went to Intel. He went to DEC. Where their paths diverged were with the demise of DEC and the fact that the hardware company didn't see the power of personal computing coming. In fact, in 1977, DEC chairman Ken Olsen said publicly, "*There is no reason for any individual to have a computer in his home.*" Perhaps the most famous last words ever spoken.

Intel was still going strong and Avi had become an entrepreneur, starting his first tech company as DEC was sold. At that point he learned firsthand the meaning of the term bootstrap, since he had very little cash to invest in the enterprise after he burned through the seed capital from his parents and his uncle's estate.

He had used the seed capital to get the minimum viable product built, and then he had self funded the development of the services. He also borrowed $100,000 from friends and advisors he had met at MIT for marketing and support, but that barely took him through the first six months after the launch of their methodologies. He later sold that initial company to Compaq and invested the proceeds in his current company.

There was a single word that stuck out from Ekaterina's talk—breakthrough. She spoke about first having small breakthrough acts, such as standing up for yourself. *I haven't done much of that in the last few months.*

He had quickly slipped into a subservient role with the Firm, instead of realizing what an honor it was to be selected as their partner in taking his company to the next level.

She also talked about how breakthroughs don't always have to be in technology. He made a quick note to himself, "Spend more time doing breakthrough thinking with the team." Ekaterina recommitted to do this on all fronts, not just in the product. He also chided himself for having poured cold water on all of Catherine's ideas over the past three days. He definitely owed her an apology.

As the TED Talk finished, he decided that he would listen to the rest of the interview on his way to the restaurant. Before he turned off his computer, he texted himself the link to the show so that he could listen in the car. He called and ordered his usual pad Thai and packed up his stuff.

When he got settled in the car, he queued up the show to the place where he had stopped listening. Ekaterina was sharing some statistics that surprised him. She said, "Half of the companies in Silicon Valley have one or more immigrants as a key founder." He didn't know that. He had never hidden his immigrant status, but neither had he been overtly proud of it. Ekaterina seemed to wear her status as the badge of courage that he knew in his heart that it was.

He had read a book last month called *Startup Nation* that reported that Israel had more companies on the NASDAQ than any other foreign country. He had also read in *The Economist* that Israel now has more high-tech start-ups and a larger venture capital industry per capita than any other country in the world. That made him even more proud of his heritage. He vowed to pick that book up again this weekend so that he could share with Amanda why shooting for a public offering should be their goal, and how his heritage could be positioned as an asset.

His attention was drawn back to the interview, which had shifted from Ekaterina's story to the book. The interviewer walked her through the main components of Zuckerberg's success—passion, purpose, people, product, and partnerships. It was a simple model and one that he believed that he could rally his executive team and the staff around.

In fact, Avi was so excited about this that once he got hold of the woman about the integrated planning process, he was going to ask if they could use this model to define their strategy. Ekaterina talked about her eye diagram, and how it helped to walk through the elements of a company's environment and resources and how they contributed to achieving your

Illustration of the concepts from Think Like Zuck, McGraw-Hill © Copyright 2013

purpose with passion, weaving both into your product. *We could certainly use that*, Avi mused.

Ekaterina talked next about the importance of finding the right mentors and how the board of directors could serve that purpose. Amanda has just talked to him this morning about finding a female to serve as an outside board member. He found himself daydreaming about getting Ekaterina on his board. He was then brought back to the moment by her thoughts on hiring. She said that you should hire for attitude not skill. She added that, "Skill can be taught, but passion can't." Avi remembered telling Catherine something similar when he met her in Milwaukee and took a chance on hiring her.

He was then surprised that the next thing they discussed was non-traditional paths to success, such as rotating people through leadership positions. Perhaps the now-infamous swap was inspired after all! He would have to remember to share that with Amanda. He was nearly at the Thai restaurant. As he took his exit off the Veterans Expressway, the host was bringing the interview to a close. She asked Ekaterina what single thought that she wanted to leave with her listeners. The author then read a quote by Henry Ford, "If you think you can or think you can't, you are absolutely right."

Truer words were never spoken! Then the last words that Ekaterina spoke before the Interviewer ended the show hit him like an arrow seeking out the center of a bulls-eye. It seemed to be just for him.

"He who dares, wins."

He was now armed and ready for his meeting with Amanda and as he pulled into the restaurant to pick up his to-go order, he realized that he was smiling, for the first time in a long time.

Chapter 8

The Beginning of the Beginning

■ ■ Tampa | Present Day | Avi ■ ■

During the course of his career, Avi had experienced many days where he knew that he was coming to the end of a chapter. He painfully recalled the last days at DEC. The writing had been on the wall for some time, and in 1992 when Avi heard Ken Olsen say in a speech, "People will get tired of managing personal computers." he knew that Ken was in serious denial and it was only a matter of time. Avi should have gotten out then.

He had that same sensation when he sold his first business. He knew before it was even time to sell. In fact, Sarah always seemed to know before he did and she would begin egging him on to think about what is next. He would always say, "I'm not finished with this yet," but she would always smile and say, "I think you are." It was maddening, but he knew she was right. He had even felt that way the day that he took the investment from the Firm.

But today was very different. I feel like today is the start of a whole new book—the beginning of the beginning. He would have to talk to Sarah about it when she got back from her trip.

Saturday morning was always his time alone. It was his time to unwind from the week and get his head cleared of business, so they could really enjoy the rest of the weekend as a family, with no distractions from work. But today, the kids were still at his in-laws and Sarah was still out of town, so even if it wasn't the tradition, he would have been alone anyway.

He had never imagined after the failure of his first marriage that he would ever fall in love again. Sarah had come into his life a year after his divorce. He was already at DEC and she was the project lead from the Finance Department on the internal implementation of Capture, the automated expense report product from AMR.

Sarah was fifteen years younger than he and when they married in 2004, even though he was already well into his 50s, they decided to have kids. This made his parents very happy. And the fact Sarah was Jewish made a huge difference, both to his parents and to him. He was embarrassed to admit that his first wife, while charming, was an atheist. He had been young and not terribly religious himself when they met. But Avi knew instinctively that the lack of faith (of any kind) as a basis for their relationship had been problematic from the beginning.

The kids loved Sarah's parents. What was not to love? Their grandparents lived on the water and they would likely take the kids out on the boat today. Avi's daughter Karina would probably spend her time on the boat texting her friends. His son Ben loved to fish and he was a great photographer. His son had shared last weekend that there were some prominent fishing magazines following him on Instagram, where he posted all of his catches. He had resisted getting a smart phone for his son, but Sarah had convinced him to get him one for his birthday, along with a Go-Pro camera, which allowed Ben to film everything that he did on the boat.

Last weekend Catherine's son Connor had come over, and Ben had produced an amazing film of him teaching some of the younger kids in the neighborhood how to catch bait and get their rods ready to catch Red Fish. Connor knew all the rules and was incredibly patient with the kids. Ben was becoming quite the film editor, setting his fishing footage to music. They had even posted the video to Connor's YouTube account, under his moniker FisherBeast.

This weekend, he started his day by walking to the local bookstore. It was a glorious day, not a cloud in the sky. It was a peaceful walk, down the long, tree-lined boulevard between the gated community where he lived and the bookstore, which was about a mile away. The walk was a part of his Saturday morning ritual, as it gave him time to think. There was something about being outside, even on a gloomy day. But here in Florida, with 335 days of sunshine, he didn't experience much gloom.

When he got to the bookstore, he went right to the business book section and was happy when he saw the picture of Mark Zuckerburg, founder of Facebook, staring back at him at eye level on the end-cap display, next to a book about Bill Gates. While both books had come out a few years ago, they were back on display in the prime space due to Snapchat's impending public offering. Facebook owned Snapchat's competitor Instagram and recently Zuckerberg had repeatedly been compared to Bill Gates in the media. Under Gates' leadership, Microsoft became known as a company that would win at any cost. From productivity apps to web browsers, any competitor Microsoft couldn't simply buy, it would crush by making a new, competing product and win by selling to its huge existing customer base. Clearly Facebook was mirroring that strategy.

He bought the book, grabbed a cup of coffee, and found a comfy chair.

The time passed in the blink of an eye and at noon he looked at his watch, amazed that he had read over half of the book. It was time to get back, as he wanted to get his honey-do list out of the way before his wife got back. He decided to walk up to the grocery store and grab the makings for dinner, so Sarah wouldn't have to worry about it when she got home.

He would keep it simple, with steak, a salad and diced, pan-fried potatoes. Couple that with a bottle of her favorite Tempranillo, a red wine from Spain, some good dark chocolate, and the dinner would be complete.

His phone beeped and he picked it up and saw a picture that Sarah had taken this morning of John and Chris' German shepherd puppy, Blitz and the puppy's aunt Aoesee, before she left for the airport. He texted back a smile and asked Sarah to send his love to her hosts. They lived close to Dallas Love Field, so she had flown Southwest. Her flight was leaving soon. He then called his father-in-law and asked if they could keep the kids one more night. Of course, the answer was always yes. He spoke to Karina and Ben, agreeing to pick them up at noon on Sunday, so they could sleep in.

He had been sick on Valentine's Day, so this would be the make-up dinner. He grabbed a mixed bouquet of roses and headed to the checkout.

■ ■ ■ ■

On Sunday afternoon, Avi had some unexpected time alone while Sarah took the kids to see the new *Surviving the Serengeti* movie. They had all loved the original movie, *Against the Wild*, which had been released directly to DVD. Avi really wanted to finish the book about Zuckerberg, so he stayed behind, offering to make his famous chickpea stew with crusty bread that evening. He had bought the makings yesterday when he was at the store. As soon as they had backed out of the driveway, Avi settled down in his favorite chair with a cup of hot tea.

Ekaterina had deftly distilled down the five business secrets of Facebook, but she didn't stop there. He loved the stories of how Zappos, TOMS Shoes, CollegeHumor.com, and Southwest Airlines had used the same five principles of passion, purpose, people, product and partnerships to succeed; each in their own industry and in their own way. While telling Zuckerberg's story, she also shared meaningful, actionable insights that anyone could use, whether inside a big company or in a startup.

His personal take-away was that since he sold part of his company to the Firm, he had stopped being a trailblazer and he had lost his entrepreneurial spirit. Instead, he had been trying to please them, doing things that were not his natural skill. He had clearly taken his eye off his commitment to change the world and was no longer driven by the soul of innovation. He lost his passion and lost sight of his purpose. He also felt he was in danger of losing the admiration and loyalty of his people and worse, that his partnership with the Firm had been totally underutilized and squandered.

With the Firm at his side, he now had the cash he needed and should look at what they could accomplish together. He was no longer forced to bootstrap his business and that was such a huge relief. But he had better speed up, as he didn't have an infinite amount of time to produce results.

He realized then that he was back in the saddle again! He wanted to talk to Amanda right away about his new perspective, and about setting up the integrated planning session as soon as possible. But first he wanted to meet with his direct reports and do whatever damage control was necessary from last week's offsite meetings. If Amanda wanted to do that together, that would be ideal.

As if she had heard his thoughts, the phone rang and it was Amanda. "Avi, I'm wanting to have our one-on-one face-to-face this coming week. I have a very busy day Monday, but could catch an afternoon non-stop to Tampa and arrive in time for dinner. How does that sound?"

Any other day, Avi would have worried about why she wanted to see him in person, but today, he wasn't concerned at all. He did a quick calendar check and saw that Sarah would be taking the kids to Color Me Mine, their favorite pottery-painting place on Monday evening to celebrate exams being over. He breathed a small sigh of relief. He could dodge the workaholic discussion for another day.

"That sounds great Amanda. Actually, I am thankful that we will have time away from the office in a more relaxed setting." he said in response. He too knew that the first step of working with her in partnership was to build the foundation for a solid, trusting relationship and was grateful that she was willing to invest the time to come to Tampa. It meant a lot to the team as well that everything didn't have to happen in New York. While they were talking, he booked a table at Eddie V's for 7:00 p.m. on OpenTable.

"I'll pick you up at AA baggage claim at 6:30 p.m.," he said. Amanda responded, "Perfect. See you then, Avi. Enjoy the rest of your weekend."

Since he now had freed up nearly two hours from his schedule by pushing his one-on-one with Amanda to the evening, he decided to see if the team could join him for an impromptu lunch. He reached out to Catherine, Jonathan, and Tim and as an afterthought, also included Jake, the CFO.

They each rearranged their schedule and agreed to join him at 12:30 p.m. on Monday at the Chart House, which was right down the Causeway from their office on Rocky Point. Their office was in the same building as the Hyatt. That reminded him that he needed to see if they had a meeting room available for next week's planning session.

The sales department at the hotel knew him well and quickly confirmed not only the meeting room and the catering and AV for the three-day session, but also booked sleeping rooms for the team. He knew the days would be long, so he didn't want them having to drive home each night.

He then called ahead to the Chart House and asked for Ryan Walker, the General Manager.

"Ryan, I have a special lunch that I would like to do today on the spur of the moment with my team."

Ryan immediately responded, "Don't worry about a thing, Avi. I will set up a special table for you by the window and take care of the menu."

He would miss the Chart House, as it was closing soon, the casualty of real estate development. Apparently, the landowner could make more from million-dollar condos than the restaurant.

He knew that Ryan and his team would land well, as they were still affiliated with Landry's, the parent company. He had discovered the restaurant seven years ago with Sarah one December evening when their favorite restaurant by the Hyatt was closed for renovations. It had been at that marvelous time of winter in Tampa when the humidity was low, the temperature was in the high 70's and the rest of the world was shoveling snow. They sat outside that night, enjoying a crisp bottle of Chardonnay and sushi, as the restaurant was experiencing a power outage so the kitchen was not able to cook anything. Ryan had introduced himself to them and apologized that they weren't serving the full menu. He even signed them up for the Landry's group loyalty club, giving them extra points for the inconvenience, encouraging them to make this their preferred restaurant. This had become their Wednesday night date night place and Ryan had become a dear friend.

Today it was a beautiful day in May, so they were eating inside, but having a long lunch with a view of Tampa Bay in the background still felt somewhat rebellious and definitely indulgent.

Yes. I am back and I dare anyone to get in my way!

Chapter 9

Zombie Logic from the CFO?

■ ■ **Tampa | Present Day | The Team and Jake, the CFO** ■ ■

Avi was the first to arrive at the Chart House and he was glad to see his favorite server, Kyle, was working and had been assigned to their table by the window. His assistant, Hernan, was also there helping him. Hernan had been with the restaurant since it had opened and always greeted Avi with a respectful hug. Hernan was Colombian. Ryan had told him that he was making sure that Hernan went with him, wherever he landed.

Avi's core team all came in one car and were happy to see that they had a table with a view. None of them ever got tired of the view of the Bay. It was such a beautiful afternoon and this was such a nice diversion. Jake arrived last and surprised them all by bringing in a big, nondescript fabric bag that you might use to bring home your groceries if you were eco-minded. He set it down on the ground next to his chair and said hello in that curious, detached tone that Jake was famous for. He fit every stereotype of the analytical finance guy. While everyone was curious about the bag, they were still a little uncomfortable with

Jake, so no one said a word. They figured that he would share whatever it was in due time.

Avi broke the ice with the team. "I want to personally apologize for wasting the team's time with the poorly facilitated session last week. I take full responsibility for allowing it to go on and on."

His apology was greeted at first with nervous laughter, then with smiles and nods. He relaxed a bit and even found himself telling the story about taking his date to *The Poseidon Adventure* in 1972. That made everyone unwind a bit, and even Jake loosened up and laughed.

Avi continued to share, "I know we have a lot to accomplish. The first thing that we have to do is re-group and come up with ideas of how to really turn up the dial on all fronts. Amanda and I are meeting tonight and we will commit resources to fund an action plan. I expect to share the details in our staff meeting."

He noticed everyone had calmed down significantly now that they knew the purpose of the lunch. Or perhaps it was the Chardonnay.

"I want the Company to build new products that will create customers who are so loyal, so addicted, and so passionate, that they would go out of their way to bring new customers with them each time they come back."

When he said that Jake nearly choked on his sushi appetizer. Jake abruptly apologized and said excitedly "Avi, I hate to interrupt, but I have a gift for each of you and now seems like a perfect time."

He reached into the bag and grabbed four copies of a book called *Zombie Loyalists* by Peter Shankman.

"The reason that I choked and what caught me off guard was what Avi had said was nearly verbatim from the inside cover of the dust jacket of the book I had bought for all of you." Jake continued, "My son, who works for the New York Times, went skydiving last month with Peter. He knew Peter from his previous firm, Help A Reporter Out (or HARO for short). Peter had just released his new book about becoming customer centric and he gave my son a signed copy."

Everyone realized that although they knew that Jake was married, they had no idea that he had a son, let alone one that went skydiving with authors!

"My son read it in one sitting and brought it to me, as he knew that I had just taken on this new role for the Firm. He told me that he realized it was a bit outside the box for me! In fact, he called me the quintessential CFO. I didn't know whether to be insulted or proud."

After a brief chuckle around the table he continued, "Anyway, he highly recommended that I read it, as it was game changing. And read it I did. All in one night in fact. With each chapter, I found myself opened to new ideas that I hadn't considered since business school." Jake took a sip of his wine and went on, with a somewhat wistful tone. "I was idealistic then, and the intellectually curious culture at Duke's Fuqua School of Business had opened up the possibilities for me way beyond just mastering finance."

He went on to say that changing corporate culture and true viral marketing were not a normal part of his CFO world, but the book had grabbed him right away when he read the introduction. In fact, he shared that he had to laugh when he saw that his son had underlined the part that said when you turned your customers into loyalists, it would seem like they were actually printing money for you.

Just twenty-four hours later, Jake had asked his son if Shankman would autograph five copies for his colleagues, which Peter had gladly agreed to do. His son had picked up the books for him on Sunday afternoon, as he knew that he was flying back to Tampa Sunday night.

Jake then admitted, "With such a radical title, I wasn't even sure if CFO's were allowed to read it!"

At that, everyone laughed, secretly shocked that he had a sense of humor. Whatever barriers they each may have had with Jake were blown away at that moment.

Jake continued to surprise them by saying, "I know now that the secret to our success will be found in being more customer-centric than our competitors." He finished his comments by committing CFO heresy by suggesting that by shifting their focus from profits to the customer would serve all their stakeholders better, including his Firm. Jake knew that was going way out on a limb, since his role as CFO had always been as the keeper of profitability.

Jake was an expert at saying no to everyone, including the Sales Department when they brought deals for him to approve. His job was to eke out every single penny possible from the expense side of the equation, often strangling the revenue generating side of the business as a casualty of that decision.

From there, Tim spoke up and shared, "I had a revelation over the weekend that Catherine, Jonathan and I need to plan a road trip to visit at least two customers that have left us in the past year. Two that we have lost in the bidding process and two that are really mad at us, due to either poor service or product issues. I want to call this the *Keeper of the Truth* tour, as I now know that the customer holds the truth of our success. I've arranged for us to leave in the morning, but we will be back in time for Avi's staff meeting on Friday. Are you guys game?" He looked hopefully at Catherine and Jonathan. It was disarming.

Catherine responded, "I'm glad to hear that, Tim. It strongly resonates with me."

Tim then asked Catherine what she thought about having a Spanish version of their product. Just as he asked the question, Hernan was refilling their water and he smiled and said "Que Bueno!" Tim then rattled off something in perfect Spanish to the table attendant.

Jonathan looked at Tim wide-eyed and said "I didn't know that you were fluent in Spanish!"

Tim just smiled and said. "There are a lot of things that you don't know about me." Instead of being smug as he might have been in the past, he said it with a twinkle in his eyes and even phrased it as a dare for the team to get to know him better.

Next Catherine talked about a radical idea she had about how they could more effectively run staff meetings to surface new ideas. "I will walk you through it Friday at Avi's staff meeting, that is, if it is okay with you Avi?" He nodded and she continued, "It is simple. Once an idea is on the table, each team member builds on the previous idea, using a technique that originated in improv theatre." Seeing the blank looks on the men's faces, she said, "I promise it will make more sense when I put it in context."

That seemed to satisfy them, but she continued by saying that she had just discovered a new improv comedy club in Ybor City and suggested that they go as a group sometime soon. At the mention of comedy, everyone agreed that it would be fun.

Jonathan was next. "I would like to revisit our pricing. In fact, I think that we should change our model from getting a license fee up front, to actually giving away the product (or charging a nominal download fee). We will make our money on the transactional revenue stream that flows from the product instead, getting our product into as many hands as possible."

Jake gave a mock gasp when Jonathan mentioned the free part of the idea. By that time everyone was totally relaxed and happy that Avi had included Jake.

Nevertheless, sensing that Jake might be a little worried at his suggestion, Jonathan turned to him and said, "It is the razor blades versus razor pricing philosophy, with the marketing savvy and viral nature of the Dollar Shave Club."

Jake broke out in a huge smile, "Got it, man!" Catherine chimed in and said "And perhaps we can look at minimizing our risk by establishing a minimum booking threshold and only pay the royalty when it has been met. That way we can still be free, but cover our implementation costs." Now it was Avi that was smiling.

My team is back.

Before they left, Jake remembered Peter Shankman's offer and wanted to share his challenge. "In addition to personally autographing each one of the books, Peter made an offer that since I bought five of his books, we can write to Peter and ask him anything that we would like to know about turning our customers into zombie loyalists." So, with a smile on his face, Jake laid out the gauntlet. "Would each of you be willing to take a look at the book this week? After you have read it, I'd like for each one to think of the one thing that you would want me to ask Peter if he were there in the room with us."

Tim turned to Avi and said with a playful grin, "No problem, we'll all just take the rest of the day off to read it!" Everyone laughed. They were really liking the new Tim.

Jake waited for the laughter to die down and added in a more serious tone, "I will pick the top question and take the winner out for a nice dinner! I have two tickets to a concert this Friday night in Ybor City. The artist is the son of friends of mine. His name is Jace Everett. You may know him as the songwriter of the theme song from *True Blood*." Tim and Jonathan both said at the same time, "I love that show!" then looked at each other and laughed.

Another layer of ice broken.

The team was definitely competitive and the game was indeed on. They all enthusiastically agreed to read it before their staff meeting on Friday. It looked like it would be a lot of fun and would inspire them to change the game dramatically.

As all of this was transpiring, Avi thought that if Jake had suggested a concert and dinner alone with one of them before today, there wasn't one of them who would have taken him up on it. Things had shifted and now he truly seemed like one of the core team. He was relieved, with a capital R. Avi was so glad that he asked Jake to join them. He silently wondered when Jake had been planning to give them the books if he hadn't been asked to lunch.

The GM of the restaurant delivered a special dessert platter he had asked the chef to prepare for his favorite guests. It included a selection of individual bites of all of their special confections, plus it was laden with fresh fruit for those "in training." Ryan said this as he looked directly at Catherine, with a smile of admiration. He told them it was on the house, his gift to show his appreciation for their business throughout the year. He said that he knew that there were many restaurant choices within a five-mile radius and he was grateful that they had selected the Chart House, especially since they were closing soon. He promised to let him know when the new location had been selected. In the interim he would be at the Mitchell's Fish Market at Westshore Mall.

As Hernan poured coffee, Jonathan said, "It is so great to feel the entrepreneurial energy flow again!" He was greeted with enthusiastic responses from everyone. "As the historic *keeper of order*, I would like to throw out an idea of doing another offsite, but this time I would like to see us do an integrated planning session. At that meeting we can take the concept of being customer centric and build a company-wide strategy around that goal. The session would yield a measurable, executable plan, from which we can derive the budget and resource requirements."

Jake had a big smile on his face about the last part and said to Jonathan "Now you are just talking crazy talk!"

Avi laughed and said "Jonathan, I already secured the Hyatt meeting space for next week, and this afternoon I had planned to call the local company that I have heard specializes in just that kind of session!"

Catherine chimed in, "Since Amanda will be here, maybe when the session is over we could go to the improv theatre for dinner. I'm sure we will all need some comic relief!"

Avi laughed and said that he would look at the schedule and see if they could fit it in. Perhaps he would even rent a small bus to take them so they wouldn't have to drive and worry about parking. As their waiter delivered the check to Avi, Jake grabbed the fifth copy of the Zombie Loyalist book from his bag and handed it to Avi to give to Amanda that night. He joked "She needs to get in on the game as well!" Everyone agreed. "Game on!" Avi added.

Avi was so relieved that the meetings last week hadn't had a negative effect on the team. Although he was a bit baffled at where all of their ideas had suddenly come from, he decided not to question them. He knew that might come off as critical, so instead he vowed just to be grateful for the fresh start. He suspected that over the next few weeks, he would hear the story behind each one's newfound inspiration and innovative thinking. He might even learn how and when Tim learned how to speak perfect Spanish!

Amanda would be so relieved to hear that they weren't upset about the meeting. In fact, he was going to tell her just to leave it in the past, as they were ready to move on and didn't need to rehash the disaster. He knew that Amanda would love the game changing ideas that seemed to be flowing non-stop from everyone!

As they returned to the office, Avi was smiling again. He thought again about the word joy and realized that it perfectly described what he was feeling.

Yes. Joy and excitement. I can't wait for Amanda's flight to arrive.

Chapter 10

Dare, Dream, Do and Disrupt

Amanda's request to meet with Avi Monday night in Tampa was motivated by the fact that she wanted to meet with him in person, versus via Skype as they often did on Mondays during their one-on-one time.

She knew that the relationships that would be forged couldn't flourish if she relied on electronics to connect her to the rest of the team. In fact, it was one of the things that she and Stephen constantly fought about, as he thought she should be using Skype or Google Hangouts to do these meetings instead of constantly flying to Tampa.

That morning, since she had her suitcase with her, rather than walking, Amanda decided to take an Uber to her office. It was located at 9 West 57th. As always, she was amazed at how easy the process was to request the car and how clean the vehicle was. She loved it that the driver handed her a mini-bottle of water as soon as she got settled. She put it in her bag for later.

She pondered how ridesharing had not only tackled the problem of making taxi rides better, but that they were reinventing driving and car usage. Her teenage son had no interest in getting his license and she had calculated that taking Uber every day for a year would be cheaper than car insurance!

The driver clearly wasn't familiar with the building, so as they got close she told him to look for the giant red 9 that was in front of their building. The building was often just referred to as 9 West and she chuckled to herself as she thought about how it should have been a gigantic red shoe in front of the building instead of the 9. She thought about sharing her joke with the driver, but she suspected that the reference to the shoe retailer would have been lost on him. She got out of the car, grateful that she didn't have to dig for cash or a credit card, since the whole payment process was part of Uber's innovation and dare she say it, their uber-customer centricity.

As she went through the revolving door, she greeted her favorite doorman with a smile before going through the turnstile. As she put her ID card into the slot, she thought, *I am so excited about this trip to Tampa and my dinner with Avi tonight. I am determined to put the disaster of the offsite behind me and move on.*

As she stepped into the elevator she was faced with the same sea of suits that she faced daily. Amanda didn't consider herself a feminist, but at the same time, she wondered why the financial services industry had so few talented women that had penetrated the executive ranks.

The elevator moved swiftly from floor to floor, depositing suits on each floor. As they reached the eighth floor, most of the men were gone and a pretty blonde in a sleeveless blue dress stepped on the elevator, holding a leather portfolio. As the young woman smiled shyly at Amanda, she was reminded of the story of her friend Whitney Johnson, who lived the real-life story portrayed in the 1988 film *Working Girl.* Like the character played by Melanie Griffith, Whitney was an attractive young woman that had started on Wall Street as a secretary. Through the same sheer grit and determination demonstrated by Griffith's character, Whitney had ended up as one of the top institutional investor-ranked analysts.

Amanda had met Whitney briefly when her firm was collaborating with the investment bankers from Solomon Smith Barney on the acquisition of a global travel firm. Coincidentally, they had met in this very building in a large room overlooking central park. Whitney had been an analyst on the Latin America market, and although she focused on media, the client had asked for her by name since some of the assets being acquired were in Central and South America.

They had become fast friends, even though there was a decade separating them. She was so proud of Whitney. She had gone on to work at Merrill Lynch as a senior analyst and had eventually co-founded an investment firm with one of Amanda's heroes, author Clayton Christiansen.

A few years ago, Whitney had written a booked titled *Dare, Dream, Do*. Naïvely, she had thought most women were following similar paths until she started talking and found that many women were not daring to dream at all, let alone "do". She had a copy of Whitney's book on her credenza in her office, in a large stack of books that she kept meaning to read. She would have to remember to put it in her bag to read on the plane.

Amanda remembered that the book talked about the remarkable things that happen when you dare to dream. She certainly understood the dare and do part of the equation, but as an investor, she found herself simply funding others' dreams and not going after her own. Case in point was working with Avi to bring about his dream. It was a delicate balance between investors and entrepreneurs, and she had sensed from Avi that he somehow felt that having the dream was more valuable than funding it. Amanda knew that in reality; they were two sides of the same coin.

Avi had accomplished so much, even though he had built the initial product using outside developers. Early on, based on Jonathan's recommendation, he had hired Paolo on contract, a young rock star designer and developer that had started programming when he was 13. His parents were Jonathan's next door neighbors in a small town called Western Super Mare in Somerset, England. Coincidentally, their first international client, Mitingu, was also using Paolo to do design and development. When Greg mentioned Paolo to Jonathan as someone that might be able to help solve a problem, Jonathan was reminded what a small world it was, as there weren't many Brits with an Italian name!

Paolo had even developed his own content management system that they used for all of their websites, which not only saved them time and money on that front, but it gave them a number of new features to incorporate into their platform for bloggers. Avi and Jonathan were so pleased that they offered Paolo equity in the Company and, also invested in Paolo's Base™ CMS platform. This was precisely why they had set aside their innovation fund. Ten percent of every dollar of revenue was set aside in an escrow account and the use of those funds were determined by the board. This meant that when they found a new initiative that the team felt strongly about, they didn't have to "rob from Peter to pay Paul," as was the norm in many companies.

He had also brought in Mary Jo to help Catherine out with the product roadmap from a technical perspective and to manage Paolo and their development partners. Mary Jo had been the lead on a security project for one of their consulting clients right after 9/11 and he had been very impressed with her technical skills and how she managed a complex and varied international technical team.

Normally the Firm wanted there to be a technical co-founder, but Avi had so impressed the Firm that they had made an exception. With Mary Jo filling the interim CIO/CTO role, and Paolo leading development, Amanda felt that it was a smart move and knew that Mary Jo would help them find a permanent person for the role before she retired, especially now that they were investing the money that could be used for a market rate salary.

The bottom line was that entrepreneurial dreams couldn't happen without the resources to bring them to bear and if the entrepreneur couldn't find another way to fund their development, launch and growth, then finding an investor made total sense. It really did take a village, and the Firm was now an integral part of that village. Now that the initial flurry of investment activity was behind them, tonight at dinner she would have to remember to ask Avi about his true feelings about their investment.

Amanda stepped out of the elevator and ran squarely into the colleague that had recommended the facilitator. Of all the people to run into, it had to be him. Of course, he asked her how it went. She decided to take a risk and be honest with him. Immediately she regretted the move. He tore into her and tried to turn the tables on her, blaming her that it didn't go well. He intimated that it was her lack of experience in being the senior partner responsible for the turnaround. She took a deep breath and gracefully thanked him for his observations and turned and went directly to her office. She sat at her desk and spun the chair around to look over Central Park. Her heart was pounding and she felt like she was about to explode.

Normally the view calmed her, but today she was just plain angry. She was upset at herself for her reaction and that she didn't stand her ground and explain the pandering of the facilitator to Jake and to her and how he had not been at all prepared. Moreover, she was angry that she hadn't done her own research about facilitator. Bringing someone in from New York was clearly a mistake and not a great cultural fit with the Tampa team.

She saw her stack of reading and four books from the top was *Dare, Dream, Do*. She put it into her bag and grabbed her folder that included the reports and articles that she wanted to discuss with Avi. She had a tremendous research assistant that had been trolling the Internet for content on innovation in the hospitality space. From the size of the folder, it looked like she had been extremely successful in her quest!

She had a couple of hours before she had to leave for the airport. She decided to call Whitney, as it had been months since they had talked. She knew that Whitney spent a lot of time on the road doing public speaking, so she was delighted when she answered the phone on the second ring.

"Whitney, you have been on my mind and on my heart. In fact, this morning I saw a young woman in the elevator that could have been you twenty years ago! I'm headed down to Tampa this afternoon to work with one of my portfolio companies and just threw a copy of *Dare, Dream, Do* into my bag to read on the plane."

Whitney was so happy to hear from her. "Amanda, when you get back we are going to have to get together for lunch. I live in Virginia now, but I expect to be in New York to promote my new book in a few weeks. In fact, since you are going to be flying today, I will send you a link to a radio show interview that I just did a few weeks ago on my new book."

"That sounds great! What is your new book about Whitney?"

"Well, you won't be surprised to learn that it is about disruptive innovation. In fact, the name is *Disrupt Yourself*. You will so enjoy it. I'll bring you a copy when we have lunch, but I think you will enjoy listening to the interview in the meantime."

Amanda was now even more excited about her trip. She heard the familiar ping that meant that she had an email, and sure enough, true to her word, Whitney had sent her the link to the interview on iTunes. She plugged in her phone and synched it, so that she could listen to the podcast on the plane. While she was doing the synch, she pulled up the table of contents for the book on Amazon, and printed it out so that she could take notes. She tucked it into her copy of *Dare, Dream, Do* and grabbed a highlighter and a pack of sticky notes, so that she could mark what stood out to her in the book.

She had an odd feeling that what she would learn from the book and listening to the interview would fill in a missing piece of the puzzle for the Company, and give her some nuggets of truth that Avi needed to step back into the leadership role and take the Company to the next level. It had a nice ring to it. dare, dream, do; and disrupt!

As she walked out of her office, she saw that same colleague standing by the elevator and wished that she could turn back around, but if she didn't leave now, she may miss her flight. She gritted her teeth and stood next to him, waiting for the elevator. He pushed past her to board the elevator first. While that little voice inside was daring her to say what was on her mind, she was smart enough to know that having the last word wouldn't be worth it.

Chapter 11

Clarity of Vision

Thankfully, Amanda's flight was on time. Avi waited in the cell phone lot until her flight showed that it was on the ground, as there was massive construction going on in the parking lots and around the terminals. Once he saw her flight number displayed on the gigantic board in the parking lot, he drove to pick her up at baggage claim. As he was pulling up, he spied her, waving to him, with her roller board bag and leather backpack in tow. He helped her with her bags and a little too stiffly, gave her a brief hug.

When she got in the car, she seemed a bit pensive. After a few moments of meaningless chatter about the weather and traffic, Avi decided to go for broke. "Amanda, what is bothering you?"

She paused as if considering whether to share or not and continued, "This morning I ran into my colleague who had recommended the facilitator for last week's strategy session. Of course, he asked how it went. When I was honest with him, he became really defensive. The rest of the day I found myself preoccupied with that, especially since I ran into him on my way out of the office as well. Plus, to be honest with you Avi, I was dreading having to talk to the team about what had happened last week. As they were pulling into Eddie V's, which was right across from the airport, Avi said, "Well then, I have some very good news to share with you."

The valet helped Amanda out of the car. With a practiced hand, Avi smoothly gave him a five-dollar bill as the valet held the door for Amanda. The maître'd ushered them directly to their table and signaled to Avi's favorite waiter. Without being asked, the waiter brought two waters and two wine glasses. Behind him was another waiter with Avi's favorite bottle of Chardonnay, which he had ordered ahead of time, to be served just slightly chilled. He didn't realize how welcome it would be to Amanda.

They stayed silent as the waiter poured the wine and quietly slipped away. Amanda promised herself that she would limit herself to two glasses, one now and one with the meal. Avi did a quick toast and then began to tell the story of his lunch with the team.

She laughed when he told the story about Jake and the books and said, "While I won't say we are close friends, I have known Jake for nearly fifteen years now and I have never known him to break ranks from his conservative, bottom-line focus!"

Amanda had to admit complete relief when she heard that there was no need to address the issue of the facilitator and the strategy session. She was happy to be able to focus on the future and not the past. It wasn't her style to dwell on the things that couldn't be changed. That brought to mind the first few chapters in Whitney's book about playing to your distinctive strengths and embracing constraints. She shared with Avi the highlights from the interview, and in particular, the notion that the interviewer had brought up that money was often the perceived competitive strength when you looked at others around you.

"Avi, last week in the offsite, you talked about the major players in the industry that have missed your vision and how you can't believe that they don't see the problem or the solution. When you said that, it made me wonder if you were doubting your genius in inventing the Toolkit. You also talked a lot about how deep their pockets were, as if that would actually translate directly into innovation."

He responded, "I won't lie to you Amanda, sometimes I just feel downright inferior when I see market capitalizations that include "B" for billions. But I've been doing some soul searching about my attitudes about funding, and I realize that with what we raised from the Firm, we are so far ahead of the game and we really are poised to disrupt the industry and lead the way moving forward by rolling up some of the other small players in our field."

Avi then said, "Back to the offsite topic, I took the liberty to contact the company here in Tampa that had the integrated planning process that I mentioned to you on the phone yesterday. They guarantee the results and provide project planning for the execution of the resulting plan. At the end of three days, they will deliver to us an executable, measurable plan." He then added, "Jake will love it! And after hearing about your friend's book, you will also love the fact that the facilitator focuses her entire consulting practice on disruptive innovation. It is like it was meant to be!"

Amanda said, "I am just thrilled Avi and I'm hopeful that this is just what is needed to move us to the next level. And by the way, you will be receiving a copy of *Disrupt Yourself* in the mail, as I ordered it for you right after I listened to the interview. Here, let me send you the link to the interview while I'm thinking of it." Amanda pulled out her phone and forwarded Whitney's email to Avi.

Avi seemed very confident, as he had called several of the Facilitator's references, including their friend Chris, and they were all enthusiastic about what they had achieved. One shared that they had accomplished, "Just 95%" of the project plan after one year. Avi had laughed at that one. *Only 95%?! Amazing!* In the small world category, their friend Chris had been a part of the facilitation for that particular session.

Another individual told him that the RapidStrategy™ session not only helped them get everyone on the bus with their new strategy, but it had actually helped them expose a contrarian team member that shouldn't have been on the bus at all. They let that person go gracefully after the session, indicating that it was clear that he did not buy into the strategy.

Avi had shared with that person, "I don't think we have anyone in that situation since we are so much smaller than you are, but it is great to hear the integrated session was an action-oriented approach." He liked that and he knew the Firm would too.

The waiter brought their appetizer and Amanda pondered the fact that Avi must have taken care of ordering in advance, so that they wouldn't be interrupted. *He was such a gentleman. Stephen had never done anything like that.*

"You know Amanda, I think our team is in the right frame of mind now, despite the failure of last week's session, so I went ahead and scheduled the integrated planning session for a week from tomorrow and secured the hotel meeting space and sleeping rooms for our executive team and their direct reports. I know it is a large expense, but I believe wholeheartedly that it will provide a return on investment. We should be able to cut our budget and planning cycle by at least six weeks, which will allow everyone to focus on doing versus planning."

Amanda made a mental note to see if Whitney would be willing to send a case of autographed *Disrupt Yourself* books for her to hand out at the offsite. Then she quickly checked her schedule and sent a text to her assistant to book her flights, coming in the day before to meet with Avi and the facilitator. She decided to stay until Friday so that she could join the team at the improv theatre Thursday night, which Avi had mentioned when sharing the details of their luncheon. She was excited!

Almost without taking a breath, Amanda turned the discussion quickly from the strategy session to Avi and his role with the Company. She started by asking him a very pointed question, "Avi, do you want to be in charge?"

He was a bit taken aback, as it seemed to be an odd question to ask a CEO, but he only hesitated a brief moment before taking a deep breath and answering emphatically, "Absolutely, yes."

Amanda paused for a fraction of a second and then said, "I know that the transition has been a bit rough and with me here, it may even feel like you are no longer at the helm, but I am here to make sure that you are ready to be in charge and ready to lead the Company to the next level. I will help you in any way I can to not only turn around the Company, but to win big!"

© marketoonist.com

Amanda knew from talking privately to Catherine that in the past that Avi had been easily distracted by new things, and while she didn't want to break that confidence, she did want to have that discussion with him. So, she decided to venture out and talk about focus with Avi.

Just as she had made that decision, Avi jumped ahead of her thoughts and said, "Amanda, one thing that I will need your help with is what the team calls "Shiny Object Syndrome." In the past, as I have seen new opportunities, instead of thoroughly researching what the new opportunity would do for us, I have gone ahead and pulled the team away from what they were focused on. I know that last week, when I pushed my idea with going with the business traveler as our target market for the new widgets, that the 800-pound gorilla in the CRM space was my shiny object."

Amanda was so pleased that he had broken the ice on the topic. All that she could do was smile and say, "You have my support Avi."

He smiled back at her, remembering the Fishburne cartoon on the topic that he had seen earlier this week. He then raised his glass and toasted, "To focus!"

They clinked their glasses and then Avi decided to share some of his immigrant story with her. He even told her about the impact that his grandmother had had on him.

After hearing about his grandfather's interment, she shared with him, "Avi, did I ever tell you that I went to the University in Warsaw? In fact, my daughter Elise has decided to go there in the fall." She paused and then continued, "Thinking of your grandfather's story, I want to share the profound impact that visiting Auschwitz and the Schindler Museum in Krakow had on me. We think of these things as historical events in time and often forget that the Holocaust happened to real people, fathers and mothers, grandfathers and grandfathers." Avi reached out and touched Amanda's hand gently, saying "Thank you, Amanda. Sarah and I just watched *The Pianist* last night, and it is one of the best portrayals of the impact of those tragic times on individuals."

Avi then decided to lighten the moment. "I heard Catherine telling someone at the offsite meeting that her daughter was thinking about the Psychology program at the University of Warsaw too. I wondered what the attraction was, but now, knowing about your mentorship of Catherine, it makes total sense."

Amanda smiled, touched by the interaction a moment ago, yet not surprised that Avi turned the conversation back to comfortable territory. Avi noticed that as Amanda continued, she seemed somewhat amused.

"Yes, there was that, but this is something a bit more basic. As soon as Catherine told me that she had a seventeen-year-old that was struggling with her decision about college, I got Elise and Veronica together for a weekend in New York City. We were fortunate to get tickets to *Hamilton*, which they both adore, and it wasn't long after that trip before they were conspiring online! They have even started looking for an apartment to share for the fall, even though they can't even apply for the program until mid-June! And be forewarned. This fall is the 200th anniversary for the University, and I'm sure Catherine will want to come over with me for the festivities in November if, no, when the girls get in!"

They laughed and the waiter was suddenly there, pouring another glass of wine. Without fanfare, Amanda politely declined and asked for a cup of tea. Avi decided to join her, amazed that they had one more thing in common. The waiter brought a beautiful wooden box with more than a dozen choices of tea. They both reached for Jasmine, laughing as their hands collided.

More ice broken.

"You know Amanda, over the weekend, I had an epiphany." Surprising himself, he related, "Over the last few months, I have tried to become what I thought the Firm wanted. Now, I realize that my value is in my own entrepreneurial spirit and how I can motivate my team to make my vision a reality." He then stunned her. "Amanda, I haven't ever told you that I see you as a true change agent and I applaud you on the changes with Jonathan and Tim. While I questioned the swap at first, I now know that it was inspired."

Amanda was touched beyond what she could express and she found when she went to speak that she was a little choked up, so she just remained silent and smiled.

Avi then turned the tables on Amanda. "What is it that you want out of your life Amanda?"

She was quick to respond, "For me, it is all about achieving pride, power, and joy at work."

Avi responded, "Joy. There is that word again. You don't know how many times over the last forty-eight hours that word has been a part of my thoughts. Continue."

"Hold that thought Avi, as I want to hear more about that. But I do want to clarify that the pride would come from seeing your firm succeed, knowing that I was a catalyst in that success. And the power I refer to is actually not my own power, but empowering your team, giving them the resources and support that they needed to win." She deftly removed the teabag from her cup, putting it in the crystal dish that the waiter had brought for that purpose and continued, "Lastly, the joy would be from forming long-term relationships with the team, and sharing their success and even sharing more of their lives and who they are outside of work. It would lead to an integrated culture of joy, not only with the team but with our customers and vendor partners."

Avi was speechless, as that mirrored what he had been thinking about all weekend, particularly the joy element. "Tell me more Amanda about what would give you joy."

She was jolted back to the moment when she was listening to Charlotte Beer's interview. It took a moment to put her words together, and when she began talking, it was slow and came out as almost a hush. Avi had to lean forward to hear her amidst the noise in the restaurant.

"For me it would be that game changing moment when I sweep everyone up into a direction that they hadn't thought of and then being able to articulate the vision in such a way that causes them to follow. That is my definition of joy."

As a woman, Avi had expected something totally different from her on the topic of joy, but was pleased at where the conversation was leading. He removed his own teabag and sat back into his chair.

He responded, "Amanda, I have to admit that I absolutely relate, although that wasn't what I expected from you!" They both chuckled, then he returned to his more serious expression and said, "I know what that feels like and I'm longing to experience that again."

Amanda admitted, "Avi, I admire your entrepreneurial energy, even in the face of the recent challenges. I went right from MIT into a corporate job and it wasn't until I joined the Firm that I had the opportunity to have an impact on entrepreneurial companies. I have to admit that I had always operated from a very analytical, detached position, similar to Jake's role."

She then decided to step out a bit, opening up even more. "You may not be aware, but I've had so many sleepless nights since taking on this role. I knew I couldn't just push you aside to do the turn around. We have to do it together. This time, I'm ready to walk hand-in-hand with you. I know it is a risk, as it definitely isn't my brief from the Firm, but I have to say that I am really excited about stepping out and breaking ranks. As a named partner, I finally have that clout and don't have to ask anyone's permission, but I still feel a little like a rebel!"

As Amanda opened up, he remembered his comment to Jonathan just a few days ago about the Firm not losing sleep and he made a note to talk to him. He didn't want to break Amanda's confidence, but perhaps he could talk to Jonathan about looking at Amanda and even Jake as a bit more human than their discussion about their roles had implied.

Avi had forgotten that Amanda had gone to MIT's Sloan School of Business, so they talked about his days at MIT, which preceded hers by about five years. They had shared a few professors, and when Avi had briefly considered getting his MBA, he had met with her favorite advisor at Sloan. Avi mentioned Benjamin as he mentioned how he found out about MIT, but he kept that part of his story short, as he didn't want to sound like he was name dropping. He quickly went on tell her about his friend who had moved from MIT to Duke, and that he was the one who had found Tim. She was amazed at how small the world really was, yet she had no idea how small it would become as the rest of the story unfolded.

Amanda then said "Can I share something personal with you?" He, of course, said yes. "You may be aware that my husband and I are separated." Avi nodded. "I want you to know that although the Firm encourages us to keep our personal life completely segregated from business, that over the last few months, I have been a bit distracted by my situation. My family is very important to me and my personal faith demands that even through the tough times, that I believe that everything works together toward the right outcome. There is a chapter in the book of Psalms that guides my life."

Amanda paused and said, "Avi, I want to make sure that it doesn't offend you to talk about my faith."

He smiled and said, "Please continue."

"Chapter 139 talks about how from the beginning of time, our Creator mapped out the plan for our lives. He is with us through the good times, the dark times and He knows our every thought."

Avi chuckled and said nervously, "That could be a bit scary!"

Amanda smiled and continued, "You know Avi, every morning before I get out of bed, I pray for peace and clarity of vision." Avi felt an involuntary shiver, remembering a similar statement with those same exact words that he made years ago in his talk with Andy in Tallahassee. "Then every night before I go to bed, I pray that He will give me the wisdom of Solomon and the favor of Joseph on all of the businesses in my portfolio, and that He will lay out the right strategies for me in all of my business dealings."

Avi shared with Amanda a bit more about his childhood days and the Rabbi telling the stories of both Solomon and Joseph. "Amanda, I have to admit that I have never actually heard anyone pray for business strategies and favor on their company!"

Amanda laughed "You know Avi, the better that you get to know our Creator, the more that you will find that He is incredibly practical and cares about every area of our lives. He also knows all of our weaknesses and gives us insight to tap into His strength."

As she finished, as if on cue, the waiter magically re-appeared. They ordered their dessert and the waiter deftly refilled their wine glasses. This time, Amanda did not decline.

As quickly as she had delved into her faith, Amanda shifted gears and confided in Avi that the partners were hoping to take the Company public by the end of next year. It was a lofty goal, but they believed that they could pull it off, and that Avi was ready. Amanda had assured them that she would see it through, with Jake by her side to lead the preparation for the road show.

Avi couldn't contain his excitement and he raised his glass to her in a toast. "Amanda, thank you for your willingness to take this journey with me." In that instant, she knew that they would truly do it together. *They would win.*

Avi then shared some of the statistics from the book *Startup Nation*. She asked him to text the author's name to her, so she could order the book. He told her that it wasn't necessary and he reached into his briefcase and gave her an autographed copy. Oh, and I also have this one. He gave her the copy of *Zombie Loyalists* that Jake had given him for her. "Jake wanted you to have this."

She laughed again, this time out loud. Jake as a customer advocate! Who knew? She would add it to her growing stack of books to read. It was a good thing that one of God's gifts to her had been intellectual curiosity! She couldn't wait to read it and to hear Jake's perspective. He had been one of their diehard CFOs, helping them to tear apart companies to be sold in pieces and parts, so it was almost funny that he was now talking about pulling the company together and refocusing on the customer. It reminded her a little of Richard Gere in *Pretty Woman*, wanting to build ships with the founder instead of breaking up the company to sell. She chuckled, mentally picturing Jake having a picnic with bare feet on a thick patch of grass as Gere had done in the movie!

She then picked up the copy of *Startup Nation*. "Avi, this sounds like a great way to position the IPO with the press. You know, it is never too early to start thinking about how to sell the success of the offering. I will bring in my favorite PR person for you to begin having this kind of discussion. You will love her."

Avi shared the concept of defining the passion, purpose, people, product, and partnerships perspectives for the company from Ekaterina's book, and told her that was the framework he had related to the integrated planning firm for their session next week.

"That is a great idea, Avi. I love the angle of putting the customer at the center of our strategy. I'm glad that both Tim and Jonathan shared that point of view. From my mentoring with Catherine, I know that she is already on board with the idea."

Avi then said, "Oh, by the way, since we talked last week, I started looking for women that we could add to the board. You know, Amanda, when you first brought up the topic, I thought it was just a diversity thing and it made me a little uncomfortable to do it just to have some sort of quota. The culture where I was raised is very patriarchal, and I have to admit that I have sometimes had the bias that men are better for executive roles than women. But then I read a report from Catalyst that said that the 500 companies with the highest representation of women on the board of directors attained significantly higher financial performance on average than those with the lowest representation of women. You know, it was surprising and compelling at the same time."

Amanda smiled.

He promised to share the target list with her by the end of the week, so they could collaborate on that and do some preliminary interviews before the next board meeting. Almost apologetically, he said that there might be a few men on the list. All Amanda could do was laugh, relieved at how different the end of her day was from the beginning, remembering her New York colleague pushing past her to get on the elevator first. He may have been highly educated, but he couldn't even begin to spell "gentleman".

As dessert was served, Avi held up his wine glass and presciently said, "Amanda, this has been a delightful night. I hope that the stresses of your day are now a distant memory."

She realized immediately that it was true and thankfully, it wasn't just the result of the Chardonnay.

"Avi, I am relaxed and happy and really hopeful, for the first time in a long time. My prayer for peace had definitely been answered!"

As Avi reached to pay the bill, he realized that he had complete clarity of vision as to where the Company was going and how they were going to get there and he couldn't wait for the integrated planning session next week.

Chapter 12

What is on your Badge?

■ ■ **Tampa | Present Day | The Team and the New Facilitator** ■ ■

When the team began arriving at the meeting room of the Hyatt for the integrated planning session, the first thing that they all noticed was that the facilitator had a badge that said, "The Medic." Beneath it was a crude drawing of an ambulance with a red cross on the side. They knew that there were many things that needed fixing in the Company, but nevertheless, it jarred each one of them to see it in black and white (and red!).

Avi thought back to his training days in the Israeli armed forces. The Red Cross ambulance reminded him of how important the medic was to soldiers. Simultaneously disturbing and comforting, it seemed somehow fitting that here they would have their very own medic to help redesign their company.

The executive team observed that this facilitator was as different from the last facilitator as she could be. She connected with each of them immediately, welcoming them and giving them a warm handshake, often clasping their hands with both of hers, as she looked them directly in the eye. She was relaxed and her smile and the twinkle in her eye were clearly genuine. And she certainly didn't resemble a medic! She was dressed in what could only be described as Bohemian attire—a comfortable black tunic with long fringe over a geometric print dress and black skinny leg pants and boots. Despite the slightly unusual attire for someone her age, there was absolutely no pretense and she looked totally comfortable in her own skin. The previous facilitator had been formally dressed from head to toe in a suit that was tailored like Daniel Craig's Brioni suit in the latest Bond movie. No one had told him that business in Florida was done in a much more casual fashion. Tampa was definitely not Wall Street.

On the table was a big sign that said, "NO NAME name tags," and a basket of oversized badges. The Medic handed each of them a badge that was made of the same material as a white board, with a removable magnet attached that made it easy to put on. They were also given a pack of five thin point, colored dry erase markers.

"Please hold off on filling out your name badges until you are given instructions." the facilitator said as each group took the badges and the pack of pens.

As they filed in, she encouraged them to grab coffee, juice, or water and some food and they would get started promptly at 9:00 a.m.

As Jake walked in, he realized that the music playing softly in the background was Bob Dylan's "The Times, They Are A-Changin'." It made him smile.

In contrast to the last meeting that just consisted of the executive team, this time each of the executives had been encouraged to bring their direct reports to the meeting. The room was quickly filling up. There were six round tables, each with six chairs. The facilitator had asked each of the leadership team to take a separate table. The music shifted to an upbeat Santana tune.

The facilitator had three other women helping her, who stood at the door greeting people, plus a quiet guy sitting at a separate small table at the side of the room, armed with a laptop and a printer. They all smiled and greeted everyone warmly. As people filed in, they encouraged the groups to split up between the six tables, doing their best not to sit just with their own work group.

Catherine had her two marketing directors with her, the Director of Product Management and Mary Jo was there, providing the bridge between product management and development. They had just gotten the go ahead to hire a CIO, but they hadn't yet started the search. She was glad Mary Jo could be here. She would continue supporting the company as the acting CTO, even after they brought on the new executive and she moved back to Scottsdale. *Amanda said it would take a village. It was so true.*

Jonathan brought his four Regional Sales Directors and his Lead Business Development Executive, who was working on the large enterprise deals, including a significant deal in China. Amanda made a mental note to introduce him to Stephen's best friend's father, the China expert.

Tim brought Tony, the Director of Client Engagement who had been the Company's first full time employee and their new Director of Operations. Nicolas from Multiplica was also sitting with them.

Jake had the Chief of Staff and the Chief Legal Counsel with him. Despite the facilitator's urging, at his table sat Peter, the Chairman of the Board, along with board members, Olivier and Chris, and Caryn, Flo and Christine from the parent company Board.

At the front table were John, Jody and Roxy, all members of the advisory board.

The facilitator knew that the team couldn't have gotten here without them, but she made a mental note to mix them up a bit with the rest of the team once the introductions were complete. With Amanda and Avi, that made twenty-eight people, not including the facilitators, seated around six tables.

As they looked around the room, each of the six tables had stacks of multi-colored sticky notes in varying sizes and shapes and a Mason jar full of black Sharpies. There was also an assortment of various types of toys on the table—building blocks, Lincoln Logs, pipe cleaners, checkers, chess pieces, dominos, and Nerf guns.

On the wall, next to the brown butcher-block paper, there was a large eye staring at them. They could tell that there were words all around the eye, but they had been covered up with 3x5 cards. Something was definitely up. It looked like they would be rolling up their sleeves and getting some real work done on the strategic plan, and even may have some fun in the process.

Over the course of the last week, it had already felt like they all worked in a completely different company. No one really knew why, but everyone seemed more focused and definitely more optimistic.

At five minutes to nine, the music changed again, this time to "Classical Gas." As if on cue, Amanda and Avi arrived. They were both already wearing the oversized badges hanging from lanyards that had their Company name printed on them. Amanda's badge said in bright pink, "Change Agent." She had drawn a graph on the top of the badge with a hockey stick line in green, the color of money. Avi's said, "Proud Immigrant Entrepreneur." He had drawn mock grass in green across the bottom of the badge and there was an Israeli flag on a flagpole with the Star of David in blue. They were both smiling. It was clear, in more ways than one, that they were in on the facilitator's game.

After they got their coffee, they quietly took their seats. The facilitator had already gotten the board and advisory board members to disburse to the other tables. In each corner of the room, there was an easel and along the wall was a long stretch of brown paper. The excitement was evident.

As the music finished, Avi got up and went to the front of the room. He welcomed everyone and jumped right into an explanation of what he had drawn on his name badge. He found himself sharing the story of his grandmother and also his trepidation of leaving Israel and coming to the US for college, arriving in Cambridge, Massachusetts just after the Kent State shootings had occurred in Ohio. Avi said to them quietly, "I thought I had left violence and conflict behind in the Middle East. You may not know that when I was young, I wanted be a politician. In 1974, Watergate impacted me deeply and it caused me to sign up for an ethics class that changed my focus. That class is the reason why our company values begin with integrity."

He also shared the story about what he had learned regarding the number of companies founded by Israeli entrepreneurs on the New York Stock Exchange and how many firms in Silicon Valley had one or more immigrants as its founders.

"I picked 'Proud Immigrant Entrepreneur' as my badge of courage and of honor, with the flag of my country of birth proudly flying. The thick green grass underneath my name signifies healthy, sustained growth, which is my vision for the Company." Avi was smiling and relaxed. He then took a red pen from his pocket, removed the nametag and wrote across the top in bold, capital letters, "HE WHO DARES, WINS."

"That is my new motto. I have to admit that since the investment in the Company by the Firm, I haven't been myself. I want all of you to know that I am committed to bring my entrepreneurial energy back to the Company. We are going to win!" With that last statement, he punched his fist in the air as a show of power.

Everyone stood and clapped as they could tell that this was not a show or a slogan that was staged. He actually meant what he said. Avi was back!

Avi then invited Amanda to join him. Everyone could tell that something had happened between them as the energy in the room was very different. They couldn't wait to hear about it. Amanda shared her background with the team, many of whom she had never met. She talked about her time with Ogilvy and P&G and then shared how the Firm recruited her fifteen years ago. Her voice choked a little when she shared, "Most of you know that I was recently promoted to named partner."

Everyone sensed from her tone that it was a very big deal for her.

She then surprised all of the directors with her next statement, "I humbly apologize to each and every one of you for not having spent time with you either before or after the acquisition. Today is a new day for all of us and I am going to make sure that by the end of the three-day session that I am able to spend time with each of you. In fact, I have asked the facilitation team to put an extra chair at each table so that Avi and I can float amongst the work teams. I don't want to be seen as the boss or the elusive partner, but instead, as my name tag says, I want to be a Change Agent, helping each of you to succeed in your roles and to truly disrupt yourselves. You will find a book on the back table that you can grab during the break that will tell you a little more about that topic. And, I promise I will know what those roles are by the time we finish this session!"

Everyone laughed at that.

Then she took the red pen from Avi's outstretched hand and took off her badge and wrote, "I'd rather you be in charge," on her badge.

"This is really important as it is a message for each of you, including Avi." She turned and gave Avi a warm smile, "Everyone has my personal commitment to help you become better leaders and to become game changers for this industry."

More clapping. Smiles broke out all over the room. No one had to tell them that this was from Amanda's heart, as she was discretely wiping tears from her eyes as she took her seat.

Then the facilitator stepped forward and gave them instructions on creating their own "no-name" nametags. She gave them ten minutes to finish them. There was a hush in the room as each of them grabbed their pens and started digging for the true identity that they wanted to share with the rest of the team.

Avi and Amanda had definitely set the bar for transparency and honesty. The facilitator watched everyone with fascination, including Peter and the board and the advisory board members, who were enthusiastically participating. The ten minutes flew by and each of the teams, led by the executives, were asked by the facilitator to stand up and share their own stories.

Jake got up first and proudly held up his badge, which said Zombie Loyalist, with a crude drawing of a zombie. An artist he was not! There were a few snickers in the room, but Jake just smiled. He said, "I recently had an epiphany that my role in Finance and Administration is actually to serve those on the front line so that you can all deliver amazing products and services to our customers." Those who had been the targets of his infamous "NO emails" anytime they asked for anything were understandably skeptical. Avi handed him the red pen and on the top of his badge he wrote "Customers First."

Jake told them, "I am not just talking about the external customers, but that each one of you in the room are my team's customers. In our staff meeting this last week, my team all made the same commitment." He stopped and smiled at his team. They couldn't be faking when everyone in the room saw what transpired between them. They had either all been taken over by zombies, or it was a new day!

Catherine went next and proudly displayed her badge, which just had two words, "Innovation Seed." She had drawn a picture of a robot that was reminiscent of the one on *The Jetsons* television show. Next to it was a seedling sticking out of the ground. Amanda stood up and gave her the red pen to add her new motto and she wrote, "YES, AND" She knew that she needed to explain that, so she shared what she and her team had been practicing over the last week in their daily staff briefings.

"In our work sessions, when anyone comes up with an idea, they are free to share it. Then the next person would have to build on that idea by saying 'YES, AND.' You can talk to the staff. The results in just one week have been nothing short of amazing. We are looking forward to sharing our new product ideas with the rest of the team tomorrow."

Jonathan almost ran to the front of the room. Everyone chuckled. His badge had the words "Go-Giver" in blue and beneath the words was a beach and a big wave. He unapologetically shared his initial reaction to the position swap with Tim. "I was literally paralyzed with fear when I thought about taking over the role as head of Sales. I didn't know the first thing about how to cold call or how to get to the decision maker or even how to close a deal. But now, I am so excited about the prospects! My team and I met last week to talk about some alternative approaches to pricing that will open the door to so much more business with our product line. We'll share our ideas in depth tomorrow."

In the space of about two minutes, his team's estimation of him shot sky high and they were proud to have him leading them. Silently, each of them vowed to teach Jonathan everything that they knew about sales. Catherine handed off the now infamous red pen and on the top of his badge Jonathan wrote "Give more value." Before he talked about his motto, he shared with the team about the picture of the beach and the wave.

"While giving value is important, I know that I need to learn how to receive as well." He looked over at Tim and admitted, "I really need to learn about sales from you, Tim, as well as from my own team of experienced sales professionals." He shifted his gaze to his team and was stunned at the looks he received in return. He continued, "The natural ebb and flow of the waves reminds me that everything is about not only the giving, but taking as well. Just as we can't survive just exhaling, we need to inhale." He then shared the core message from *The Go-Giver.* "Giving more in value than we charge for our product will help spawn Zombie Loyalists and make the Company more profitable as a result. I believe this with all of my heart." He smiled at Jake and said, "I want to thank you publicly for seeing that both finance and legal could really help us increase sales if we work as a team, rather than being in an adversarial position."

Tim was the last of the executive team to share and his badge simply said, "Embracing Truth." That raised a few eyebrows, as it seemed obvious that everyone would want to do that. Tim had always been a bit of an odd duck, somehow superior to all of them due to his old money heritage. With his promotion, they were all fearful that this attitude would get worse rather than better.

Tim started his story with this, "For three days last week, Catherine, Jonathan, and I went on a road trip, visiting customers. Not our favorite ones, or the ones that as VP of sales I would have chosen. That would have been self-serving, simply to prove to them what a great guy that I am."

The room was so quiet you could hear the proverbial pin drop.

Tim swallowed hard and continued. "We visited two customers that had cancelled our services, as well as two that we had bid on but lost to a competitor and two of our current customers that were really mad at us. No, let me correct that. Actually, they were mad at me." His direct reports were shocked, yet happy at his humble declaration.

"Those customers are the keepers of the real truth for our Company. I learned more in those three days about how the Company should operate than I did getting my MBA, and certainly more than I understood in my years in sales." What Tim said next was totally unexpected. "During that time, it had been all about me and making my quotas. Now I realize that our clients are what is really important."

"The six stick men on my badge are a reminder to me of what we had learned from those six customers. And while those customers had all been men, I know from spending time with Catherine, that there is much to learn from understanding the female perspective as well." With that statement, he glanced over at Amanda, who was smiling broadly at him, and giving him an affirming nod. He continued, "In fact, I learned before our trip that more than 66% of all trips booked on our system are planned by women, so we should all spend more time paying attention to our female customers and prospects, and what they have to say about our product. They are also the managers of the various venues and events we are targeting with our new widgets and plug-ins. If you don't know what a widget or a plug-in is, you can ask Jake. We have thoroughly explained it to him!"

Everyone laughed in response, including Avi, remembering how silly it was to preempt Jake in the previous meeting. Jonathan then handed the red pen to Tim and he wrote the words "DEFY GRAVITY" on the top of his badge.

"I have to share with you that when I was a kid, my mom drilled into me that I could do anything that I set my mind to. I always knew that I was a winner. She helped me understand that, even when I lost a football game or a tennis match." Tim was now visibly choked up. "My mom had a stroke recently and even though she survived it, she is in a wheelchair and it feels like we have lost the person she once was." He paused and then said, "If she were here, she would ask me to apologize if I have come off as arrogant to you." He looked around the room slowly. "Please accept my apology."

He stopped and took a drink of water. There were many in the room, men and women alike that were dabbing their eyes with their napkins. The maturity that it took to make that admission belied his twenty-nine years.

Tim finished by boldly saying, "Now that I am armed with the learning from the keepers of the truth, and I know from Catherine, Jonathan, and Jake the true value of being a part of a team. We can now defy gravity. Together we will reshape the Company to focus on the customer, understanding the value that our customers need to get from our product and from our service."

Everyone not only clapped, but rose to their feet. The facilitator watched with interest as Amanda, their Chairman Peter and Chris and Olivier all exchanged a thumbs-up across the room. She knew from talking to Amanda that they had been consulted when Jake wanted to make the swap and they had all expressed some concern over his previously arrogant attitude.

The members of Tim's new team had a much greater respect for him after hearing the story behind his badge and his motto, and they couldn't wait to finally work as a team.

The facilitator announced that they would take a quick break. The music this time was "Fly Me to the Moon" by Frank Sinatra. Even after individuals left the room, they could be heard humming the catchy, upbeat tune. When they returned, the rest of their team, including the board and advisory board members went through the exercise.

Peter shared about his shift from the travel industry to the Red Cross and talked about how grateful he was to stay involved in travel. Chris shared stories from his early days in the telecoms industry and how he came to retire from his CEO/Chairman position in his early fifties. Olivier talked about his days at Unisys, teasing Avi a bit about the earlier rivalry with DEC and the entrepreneurial spirt that eventually led him to leave the tech giant. John shared about his big entrepreneurial wins and his failures and the joy that his teaching gave him with young entrepreneurs. Jody shared his time in international telecoms, as well as his experience over the last decade supporting entrepreneurs, including Avi. Roxy shared how he and the facilitator had worked together for more than a decade and how Catherine had convinced him to come out of retirement in his late '60s. Flo shared her story about meeting Amanda during the acquisition of her company and Christine talked about her time as President of LasVegas.com, having been hired by the facilitator to be a part of the launch team and that she and Avi's wife had met at a telecoms company nearly 17 years ago. The world was getting smaller by the day.

The team was warmed by the transparency that each of the executives showed. They matched the honesty and openness in each of their introductions. By 11:00 a.m., everyone had taken their turn and there was a sense of wonder and amazement in the room.

Music played softly in the background. The facilitator stood up and for a long while was very quiet. She just looked at each one and smiled. With some she connected eyes and nodded. Something deep had transpired and she just wanted to soak up the feeling in the room. It was special. Then she asked them all to close their eyes as she played "Suite: Judy Blue Eyes" by Crosby, Stills & Nash. She asked them to keep their eyes closed for at least a few minutes and think about what they had just heard from their colleagues. The good, the bad, the ugly, the hopeful, and the challenges.

She reminded them that this was a rather long song, about seven minutes in all, and that if they needed to take a break, to do so quietly. To be honest, she wasn't exactly certain why she had chosen a song that would eat up so much time on the agenda. She prayed that there was a message in it for more than one person in the room. When the song was over, not a single person had left the room and everyone was quiet, many heads still bowed.

She stood back up and said, "A part of me wants just to send everyone home. In my nearly twenty years of strategic consulting, today I saw more progress in the first ninety minutes than most teams made in the full three-day session. We have done more than twenty-five of these sessions for companies big and small, with over 150 people in the room and as few as four, but this one was truly exceptional."

She continued, "I picked that song for one reason. First, it is one of the most incredible works of harmony in modern pop music and harmony is a critical part of how companies work together. A bit of music trivia: you may not know that Stephen Stills wrote that for his ex-girlfriend, Judy Collins. She had piercing blue eyes and had pierced his heart by falling in love with an actor, Stacy Keach."

After a short pause, she went on, "Every hour of every day, we get to choose if we are going to stick with what is hard or if we are going to walk away. When we choose to do the hard work, and stay and work through challenges, the rewards are great. The harmony is amazing. While things didn't end well for Judy and Stephen, I can tell you that the prognosis for this group is equally amazing to the harmony in that song. What you are doing here will be legendary and you will leave a legacy." She continued, "If this had been a battlefield and I was indeed the medic, at this juncture, not only would I have patched up all of the wounded, but we would have just sent the enemy packing and declared victory! I have never seen this kind of trust and radical collaboration even on the last day of the three-day workshop. In fact, we've never seen it in any of the ventures where we have been brought in to help."

For some reason, that statement gave Catherine goose bumps.

The Medic then erased that name from her badge and changed it to "The Business Designer." She then said, "It is clear that you no longer need a medic. I'm here to help you design your future and to help each of you become a game changer."

She also smiled slyly and said "Avi, you remind me of someone that I knew earlier in my career that had talked about planting seeds of innovation. I have a feeling that you will soon be planting some new seeds." Now it was Avi that had goose bumps. Catherine also shivered, even though it was warm in the sun where she sat by the window in the meeting room. *It was like the Business Designer had sat in on their initial conversation back in Milwaukee.*

The Designer went on to say, "This is such an extraordinary team and you all have an amazing opportunity to really change the name of the game. In fact, because of that, I feel like my role is changing! I am going to add something to the top of my badge." She wrote in bright purple, "Birthing Game Changers." Then she joked, "Perhaps I should have changed my title to 'Company Midwife!'" She reached out for a tissue and erased the ambulance and replaced it with a domino with six dots. They figured they would hear more about that later.

They took another quick break and then jumped into next exercise. The Designer handed each person a stack of sticky notes with their initials in the upper right corner of each page. On each note, there was a description of the various tasks that needed to be done within the Company. She then drew a big grid on the Butcher-block paper with a big black marker, marking off the square in the lower right. Across the top she wrote the words LOVE and HATE. Down the left side, she wrote the words DO WELL, DO BADLY and HAVEN'T TRIED.

She explained, "Each one of you need to take the individual sticky notes from your pad. Then place each one of the notes from your pack in one of the five squares, intersecting the combination that best describes how you see yourself."

She described the exercise and gave them some examples of how to rate each task based on things she had experienced in her own work. She saw many of the team nodding and said "I think you get the drift. I crossed off the one on the lower right because you should never want to try something that you hate."

"Once you are done, the rest of the team will look at where everyone has placed themselves. I know that there will be many surprises and some might even challenge where you have placed yourself. Don't be shy! Once we are done, the executive team will then take turns and talk through what each of them have learned about their team. Have fun!"

This time, the noise level rose very quickly and the energy level in the room climbed right along with it. They were off! The Board and Advisory Board sat this one out, but enjoyed watching what unfolded. The exercise was very revealing to everyone. The stickers had words such as Financial Modeling, PowerPoint Presentations, Board Documents, Business Plan, Presentation, Cold Call, Managing People and Public Speaking. Each person got to decide whether they loved the task and did it well, or that they did it badly (or never tried it). It was eye opening to see that some things that they did well, they actually hated.

Catherine caught herself initially putting many of her stickers closer to the DO BADLY line and at the very moment of her self-realization, Tim, who was standing beside her quietly told her, "Madame, you are not doing yourself justice," moving her Product Management up to the top of the DO WELL line. She quickly adjusted the rest of her notes, boldly ignoring the little voice inside her head telling her that she was not good enough.

As normally happened in this exercise, particularly when it was done with entrepreneurs, no one put any stickers in the "Hate and Do Badly" grid. That is obviously a bad place to be. In a small company, however, there are rarely enough employees to have people in jobs that they hate and do badly. Before they finished, the Designer had them add one more dimension. She gave them each a page of red circle stickers and one of green. They were like the price stickers you would use at a yard sale.

"Go back to your sticky notes and put a green dot on those things that energize you and a red one on the ones that drain you. If you are neutral on a task, then you don't have to use a sticker." More noise! Most of them were amazed to find that some of the things they hated but did well, actually energized them. It didn't seem like that could be possible.

The Business Designer explained, "Our primary jobs should include as many 'love, do well' items as possible. If there are tasks that are needed that fall into the 'love, do badly' sector, then we need to seek training or mentoring in that area, or perhaps to be a part of a project team where that skill is needed. For those things that we hate, but do well, if they energize us, they can be a part of our responsibilities, but should never be a core part of our job. In fact, the best place for those people is to manage others doing that task or to be the one managing an outsourcer of that function."

The young man that had been sitting at the table with the laptop got up and quietly took pictures of the grid and then used his pen to mark some things on the sticky notes before taking them. Then he quietly went back to work, presumably documenting the outcome of the exercise.

The rest of the day sped by. It was clear after their working lunch that they were focusing their efforts of the strategy session on becoming totally and completely customer-centric as an organization, serving both the internal customer and the external customer.

After lunch, the Designer showed a fun, energizing video about dominoes and the amazing impact that just one domino, properly placed and aimed, can have when pushed. She called the video, "Be the Domino." The exercises that afternoon not only clarified their strategy, but it taught them new skills that could be used on a regular basis.

The Designer loved watching the board and advisory board members interact with the team and with Amanda and Jake. It was always a bit of a tightrope to have an entrepreneurial board mesh with the investor's team. She made a mental note to share her observations with Avi.

Catherine's favorite exercise was the IS and IS NOT methodology that she knew would help them in product and service definition. They not only listed what a product or service (or initiative) included, but they also expressly stated what it did not include. This removed any ambiguity from what they were discussing. When coupled with the "YES, AND" methodology that Catherine had shared, it would be incredibly powerful. She could hardly wait to get her entire team trained on this new way to approach product definition.

By the end of the day, they had articulated a clear vision statement, with measurable and attainable objectives for each part of the Company portfolio. They had also outlined the key initiatives that were necessary to complete to achieve their goal of shifting to a Customer Centric culture. For each one, they had outlined what success looked like.

It was amazing the clarity that was now coming so easily to everyone, especially since the teams were all intermingled, instead of being organized by business discipline. They used a very simple outline for each objective, such as the launch for their new curated recommendations widget project, both the standard version and the Spanish language version.

Catherine was beyond thrilled that Nico would be on board to help them launch the new Spanish language product. Nico was sitting at the table with Tim and Mary Jo and it was clear that they had all connected.

Amanda was pleased to see Nico and Mary Jo talking about how they could work together, and she wrote a note in her notebook to talk to the two of them about a couple of her other portfolio companies that were also wanting to tap into the US Hispanic community.

Next, the Designer asked Nicolas to come up and explain the model that his firm had developed for the Company. His firm had recently entered the US from Spain, and had asked Nico to lead the US market entry. The model focused on how to hold persuasive conversations with prospects and customers.

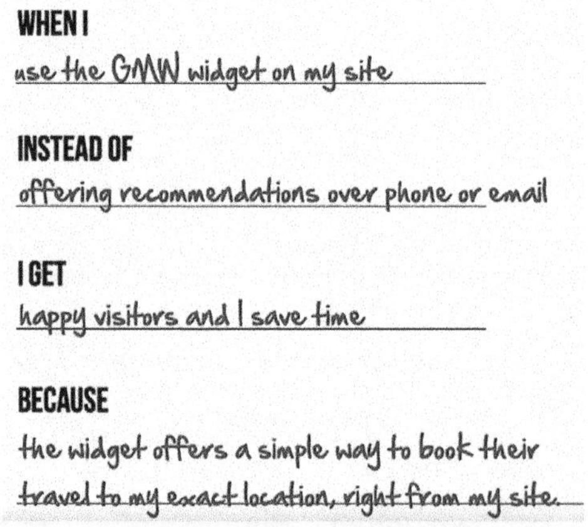
WHEN I
use the GMW widget on my site
INSTEAD OF
offering recommendations over phone or email
I GET
happy visitors and I save time
BECAUSE
the widget offers a simple way to book their travel to my exact location, right from my site.
Multiplica model

They could use this model for each of their target audiences, including the frequent traveler, Avi's favorite market! This one was for the venue managers who would use their tool on their own sites.

They had also talked through the issues of company structure and culture, including talking about some elephants in the room that had been barriers to success in the past.

The Designer wrote each one down on a dark pink sticky note and put them on a poster on the wall with a picture of a parking lot.

"Throughout the day tomorrow and again on Thursday, anything that comes up that doesn't fit in the agenda, we will put on a sticky note on the 'Parking Lot' on the wall. Anyone can add to the 'Graffiti Log' with whatever they want to say. The dark pink sticky notes are reserved for things that need urgent attention. We

Parking Lot

Graffiti Log

call those 'Tiger Team' ideas." The Designer saw a few blank looks, so she asked Avi to come up and join her.

Avi stood up and right on cue added, "In military security work, a Tiger Team is a specialized group that tests an organization's ability to protect its assets by attempting to circumvent, defeat, or otherwise thwart that organization's internal and external security. We are going to put together a small team that will be dedicated to solving any issues that come up in this session. In each of the conference rooms around our office, we will be putting these two posters on the walls. At the end of each meeting, we want you to do the same thing for your own department or project issues."

Catherine had an enormous smile on her face, grateful that their ineffective meetings would become a thing of the past.

The Business Designer wound down the day by telling them that the next day would be devoted to defining the complete list of tasks involved in implementing the various initiatives, including the people, process and tools needed. "It will be grueling, and for those of you who are mothers, it will resemble the birthing process at times, but I urge you to stick with it. The results are worth it."

She then posted the following image in a big laminated poster on the wall, sharing that, "This is a graphic is one of my favorites. The Stanford Advanced Project Management Group and the Project Management Institute jointly developed this model, no doubt inspired by the Golden Gate bridge. We have used this model to guide over 200 projects for ninety clients over the last twenty years."

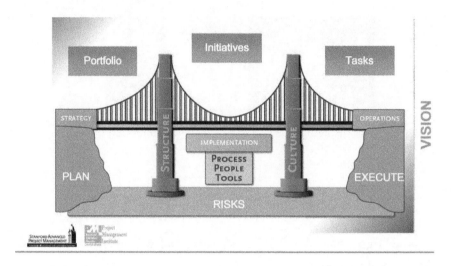

"I know that some of you are much more comfortable on the planning side of this bridge. Others only feel comfortable at the task level, getting things done that are clearly defined. My goal as a facilitator is to get you to meet in the middle, and to get everyone comfortable with the interdependencies between each of you. When I first started consulting twenty years ago, I thought that VISION was on the planning side of the bridge, but I know now that it can only happen with those that know how to execute. The plan that will result from the next two days will show all of you the way forward. And Mike," pointing to the guy at the laptop, "who is known amongst us as 'the Survivor,' will be with you every step of the way over the next six months to make sure that this is not just a written plan but a living one. He will be with you onsite several days a month as your program manager to keep everything moving forward and you will have regular calls to talk about progress, as well as the inevitable roadblocks. He will share with you during your time with him that if you are determined, you can beat anything that comes at you."

Mike smiled at the facilitator and then said to Avi, "Thanks so much for having us. Although it would be much better doing this at a time of year when I can enjoy the warm weather in Florida as the snow begins falling in Colorado!"

Everyone laughed and Avi saw that those that were from Colorado made a note to connect with Mike at the next break to plan a ski outing with him.

She also added, "One departure from our normal methodology is that Avi asked me to look at the strategy and the initiatives that supported that strategy from a lens known the Five-P Perspective: Passion, Purpose, People, Product, and Partnerships."

As she talked about those things, she removed the 3x5 cards from the eye diagram, revealing some of the concepts that they would dive into tomorrow. Those sitting close to the eye saw that it was from a book called *Think Like Zuck*. "Throughout the day on Wednesday, we will capture the complete list of interdependencies, as well as the timeline, in a process that I promise will boggle your minds."

While it was a lot of intense work and would require that everyone stay focused, she said that by the morning of the third day they would literally have a 500 to 600 line, integrated project plan. They would spend an hour reviewing the draft plan Thursday morning and agreeing upon the plan in principle. Clearly, there would be some things that required that they go back to the office and ask others to clarify or that they would need to talk to external suppliers and partners and even the "keepers of the truth."

"Within a week, with the Survivor's help, you will actually start on 'day one' of the plan, kicking off the initiatives company wide."

The Survivor added, "No wasted motion!"

The Designer finished by saying, "On the morning of the third day, we will talk about the risks that you may face, both internally and externally and the Survivor will facilitate the group in coming up with risk mitigation strategies for the top threats. He may even share with you the story behind his name tag. He seems quiet now, but get him started on risks and you won't be able to shut him up!"

Everyone laughed. They couldn't wait to dig in. She told them that it was nearly 7:00 p.m. and it was time to wind down. She asked them all to turn around. At the back of the room was a table laden with healthy food, individual half bottles of wine with twist off caps, bottles of imported and craft beer, and water, both still and sparkling. There were also brightly colored insulated bags with the words, "I am a game changer" on the one side of the bag. On the other side was a black and white picture of a chessboard with dominos placed where the chess pieces would normally be. Inside each bag was a blank spiral notebook with the same phrase and picture on the cover, plus a very nice rollerball pen.

She encouraged everyone to grab a bag and fill it with whatever they wanted to eat and drink and go back to their rooms. "If you forgot to pick up your copy of *Disrupt Yourself*, pick it up now. I suggest that you think about everything you have learned today about your peers and about yourself. The notebook and pen in the bag are for you to write down your thoughts and to begin contemplating the initiatives that are key for you and your team to achieve the stated strategy. Get a good night's rest, as there is still much to do. Tomorrow is going to be a very long day. Congratulations again on how much you have accomplished."

She saw Roxy get up and go over to Mike and the two men hugged. She was sure that Roxy was remembering the many integrated planning sessions they had done together before Roxy left them for his own entrepreneurial venture. So many great memories. Chris then joined them and she hugged them both as well.

Tomorrow is going to be a great day, thought the Designer. As she waited in line for the team to get their dinner, she pondered with a smile, *I wonder if Avi had made the connection yet.*

Chapter 13

The Business Designer

As the team was grabbing their bags, Journey's, "Don't Stop Believing" was playing softly in the background. Amanda had a huge smile on her face and she went over to Avi and said, "Today exceeded my expectations in every way. Thank you so much for your role in making it a success."

"You're welcome and I wholeheartedly agree," replied Avi.

The executive team had hung back as their teams went back to their rooms bag in hand, finally taking out their phones to check messages. Before each one left the room, they took turns shaking both Avi and Amanda's hand, thanking them for making this happen.

Those who had been invited by their bosses told them how grateful they were to be included in this process. One even said to Avi, "You know sir, you will never know how impactful getting a seat at the table is in my life at this particular moment." Avi made a mental note to spend more time with him tomorrow to get to know his backstory, as he was certain that there was something significant behind his remark.

As he saw the smart phones, Avi realize that throughout the day, he didn't see a single person texting today. Other than during the scheduled breaks, no one left the room, even to go to the bathroom. He was happy and as the facilitator and her team gathered their things and their bags with dinner, he thanked each one for an extraordinary day.

As he shook the facilitator's hands, she quickly reached out and said, "Avi, I am going to give you a big hug and by the way, give my regards to Sarah."

He noted the twinkle in her eye as she said goodnight and now he was totally stumped. His memory had been bad before, but now he was really confused. He obviously knew her though his wife, but he thought Christine was the connection. He would ask Sarah later.

The board and advisory members were the last to leave, and the facilitator thanked each one personally for their candidness and their engagement today. They each grabbed their bags and their books and headed upstairs, tired but exhilarated. Avi saw Christine give the facilitator a warm hug.

After making sure that the room was ready for Wednesday's early start, the facilitator left with the rest of her team and said goodnight to each one as they got off on their floors. Even though she lived just fifteen minutes away, Avi had gotten her a beautiful room overlooking the bay.

She put her things down and then decided to get comfortable. She looked at herself in the mirror, taking in the Bohemian look that her personal stylist Wendi had insisted that she adopt for this meeting. When she had turned fifty, she had had a complete makeover and now fully trusted her stylist, even when she came up with crazy recommendations like this one. Wendi knew that no matter what she thought that she should wear to be politically correct with her client, it had to be totally comfortable. She didn't want to be self-conscious. She had to be totally centered on them to be effective in her role as the Business Designer. Tomorrow she would lose the boots. She already had a comfortable outfit laid out that would look great with the stylish Crocs sandals that she had packed. Wendi would approve.

She thought about Avi and his comments about the Tiger Team earlier. It had been such a perfect complement to what she had been saying. Personally, she had forgotten the origin of the term, and his time in the military in Israel that would have given him that very intimate perspective. Her faith in the Grand Designer of business signaled that none of this was an accident. As she got ready for bed, she reminisced.

■ ■ Dallas | 1987 | The Business Designer ■ ■

She had been in her corporate role for five years and had just been selected to head up a new venture to provide automated expense reporting to corporations. Before her thirtieth birthday, she had led the acquisition of Capture, a UNIX based tool that had been developed by a group in California.

Her boss' boss was Max Hopper, who she knew had been one of Avi's heroes. Max had written the prologue of her first book, eCommerce Pioneers, the story of the Global Distribution Systems. He had passed away a few years ago, so the Business Designer hoped that Avi had been able to meet him while he was still alive. Knowing his fascination with Max, she had gotten an autographed copy of his famous article from the Harvard Business Review from Max's widow, Jo, and was going to give it to Avi at the end of the three-day session.

Capture had been her first startup, but she would not have considered herself an entrepreneur at that point. She was definitely an intrapreneur. She enjoyed the security of a regular paycheck and had significant resources available to her to move the company forward. She would never forget asking the company's CEO for the multiple millions needed to complete the acquisition of Capture, the startup tech company that had set out to change the way that expense reports were processed in large companies. They had kept the name of the product when they had acquired the assets.

It had been a heady experience for her to sit in the small room with all of the executives that literally sat between her and the CEO. He had begun by asking questions about the project according to the proper hierarchy, but quickly realized that she was there because she had put the deal together.

So, Bob Crandall had begun talking directly to her, bypassing all of her superiors.

Against all odds, after completing the acquisition and integrating the product into their reservation system environment, they had signed three very high profile beta test clients, Sun Microsystems, Unisys and DEC. Avi had been the key contact at DEC, but it had been Sarah, who was now his wife, that they had worked with most closely. She had never actually met Avi face-to-face, which was why he hadn't yet made the connection. She would have thought that her name would have given her away, but it didn't.

In those days, there was no such thing as a User Experience (UX) specialist. Developing with the user in mind was a totally new concept. She thought back to the day when Bob Crandall, the CEO of AMR, had come over to their office to see a demo and in his gravelly voice had said that it was, "As user friendly as a scorpion." She didn't know it then, but that moment sealed their failure on that front and from that point forward, she began her quest for serving the customer first and foremost.

It wasn't long after, that she had gone into the CEO's quarterly staff meeting, prepared to provide an update on the launch at DEC. When he came to her time on the agenda, before she even opened her mouth to speak, he had said, "Capture. Is that still around? Shut it down." Then he summarily had gone to the next item on the agenda. Stunned, she had started making a list of all the things that she needed to do to shut the business unit down, including letting the team go.

Next to her was one of the SVPs of the company. He wrote on his yellow legal pad the words, "Calm Down." She wrote on her pad, "But it was three years of my life!" He leaned over and wrote the word "only" slightly above but between the words "was" and "three."

She knew that she had found her mentor to get her through the tough days coming when she had to deal with nearly ninety displaced employees. In fact, as the meeting wound down, it had been her mentor who had told her that the first thing that she needed to do was to call Sun, Unisys and DEC before they heard the news from anyone else. "Customers first, always." he said. As he was saying that, she saw the CEO walking directly toward her. He stopped and said,

"Listen, we shut down Capture because it was a failure. If we thought you were a failure, we would have shut you down."

She knew that Crandall didn't have to take the time to say that to her and she was grateful. She now knew that being a game changing intrapreneur on this project had been her "graduate school," preparing her for her days as an entrepreneur some twenty years later when the safety net of a corporate paycheck would not be there.

■ ■ Tampa | Present Day | The Business Designer ■ ■

She then shifted her thoughts to her radio show, which she had launched in 2009 to provide executives with insights on innovation, growth, leadership and entrepreneurialism. One of her favorites was an interview with Ekaterina Walters who then played an intrapreneurial role at Intel. The interviewer had worked on a skunk works project at Intel in the early 2000 timeframe and she had shared the story on the interview with Ekaterina:

"I met the design team for the Pentium 4 chip when I was consulting with a major travel company in the Midwest and they asked if they could hire me for a half day to learn about travel technology. I had responded, 'Sure and the other half of a day, you can teach me how to build a chip!'"

She and Ekaterina had laughed at how ludicrous both the question and my response were, although mine was preposterous by design. Shortly after their first interview Ekaterina had left Intel and had founded her own company, which had already been acquired. She was now a brand evangelist for that company. She would soon be interviewing her a second time about her new book about storytelling.

She looked forward to taking the team through Ekaterina's eye model the following morning. With that thought, she decided to forego eating and instead got ready for bed.

She got into bed and grabbed the book on the bedside table and her favorite rollerball pen. The book was *The Freaks Shall Inherit the Earth* by Chris Brogan.

She had discovered Chris about six years ago when she decided to add social media and networking to her expertise in the multi-channel distribution world.

He was a pioneer in the space and to this day, she belonged to his Owner Mastery Foundation Group (irreverently referred to as OMFG) online on Google Plus.

The sub-title on the book was *Entrepreneurship for Weirdos, Misfits and World Dominators*. On the back cover, another of her favorites, Seth Godin, had commented, "This book is pure Brogan. Helpful, excited, practical and willing to challenge both the status quo and our deepest fears."

She was halfway through the book and the empty pages at the back were no longer empty. Like she did with nearly every book she read, she pulled out the truths that grabbed her and made notes with her favorite pen about how she would apply them—sometimes to her clients, and other times to her own company. It was like a medic stockpiling medicine for her patients.

She read for a while and as she felt her eyelids get a bit heavy, she set the alarm on her phone and turned off the light. Her last thoughts were that she would have to give Avi a copy of Brogan's book and tell him about OMFG. Plus, she had to remember to ask her executive producer, Pattie, to check to see if Chris would agree to be on the radio show. The Business Designer fell asleep knowing that she would dream about status quo busting and world domination!

■ ■ ■ ■

After the Business Designer and her team left, Avi suggested that Amanda and the executive team grab their dinner and just sit and talk a bit before going back to their rooms. He wanted to hear their feedback about today while it was fresh in their minds. While he enjoyed their engagement throughout the day, Avi was glad that the board and advisory board members had gone to their rooms, as he wanted the team to be totally candid about their feedback. He made a mental note to set up time with them to get their impressions, although he felt quite certain that each of them would share them with him over the course of the next two days.

There was a grouping of couches in the corner by the window, overlooking the bay. It was twilight now, but they could see the lights on Rocky Point and the glow of the Chart House. There were side tables and a coffee table where they could set down their bottles and plates.

After they got settled, Catherine commented, "What a change from the session a few weeks ago." She observed that the facilitator had consistently looked each of her people in the eye as she spoke, making each one feel special.

"In fact," Jake added, "it seemed like that other session was months ago." He then smiled and told them that he had another present for them. They all laughed as he grabbed his large cloth bag, obviously filled with more books.

Tim said what they were all thinking, although he said it in a perfect Castilian Spanish accent. "No más libros Jake!" He had thrown up both hands dramatically.

They all laughed and Catherine thought about how irritated she would have been with Tim, had they not had the time on the road together. She surprised herself that she had actually taken a liking to him, considering how she had felt about him when they first met.

This time Jake pulled out a book that was a much better fit to his role. It was *Accounting for the Numberphobic*. There were a few groans, but by now, Jake knew they were in jest.

Tim had opened the book to the introduction and was reading some of the quotes from people that the author had interviewed about how they felt about financial statements.

Tim said "I can relate to this one! *I'd rather spend the weekend listening to my mother-in-law!*"

Everyone laughed.

Jonathan jumped on the bandwagon and keying off Tim's first statement in Spanish, in an overstated British accent, he read the one that said dramatically, "*I love reading my financial statements. I also love getting a flat tire on the highway in the pouring rain at 2:00 A.M. and getting my wisdom teeth extracted.*"

More laughter. They were clearly overtired.

After it died down, Jake told the team, "I realized that in order for everyone to understand why I have been so tough on you in the past about budgeting and performance metrics, I needed to invest the time to help each of you understand the tools the Firm uses to measure its portfolio companies." Seeing their horrified and exhausted looks, he laughed and told them, "Not to worry, we aren't going to do it tonight! But I did come across this book and I felt that the author had succeeded in simplifying the basics of financial statements and even made it a bit fun. I loved the graphics that likened financial statements to dials on a car dashboard."

Amanda took that opening to share her announcement with the executive team. "This is very timely Jake. I'd like to share with everyone that at our recent partner meeting, the Firm decided to take the Company public early next year. To do that, you will all have to be not only conversant on how your departments are running, but you will need to be completely comfortable with the key elements of the IPO packet, that's, Initial Public Offering, for those that don't know."

Avi was grinning ear-to-ear as the news sunk in with the rest of the team. He had already had more than a week to embrace the idea. They were each trying to figure out the implications and why the financials were important for them.

Amanda thanked Jake again for stepping up and getting that ball rolling and then shared one more thing about the IPO. "The Firm also voted on granting the leadership team equity in the Company, effective today. Jake will be reviewing the information about your shares later in the week and should be able to answer all of your questions."

Jake told them "By the way, if you want to ease into the book, you can listen to a radio show interview with Dawn, the author, from a show that was broadcast on BlogTalkRadio. I will share the link with each of you, as I am on their email list."

As he said that, each of them looked wide-eyed at Jake, then looked at one another, with revelation in each of their eyes. Nearly simultaneously, each remembered that they had gotten an email notification of that same interview the previous Friday and for one reason or another, they had ignored it.

Tim then said, "Did the Business Designer's voice sound familiar to anyone today?"

It was then that everyone realized that she had never given her name or even said the name of her company. She didn't hand out business cards, as would have been customary and had certainly never mentioned that she had a radio show. But at that moment, they all knew that the interviewer and the Business Designer were one and the same.

She had been such a refreshing change from the self-absorbed facilitator in the previous session that no one had thought anything of the way she had handled the introductions, keeping her name out of any discussions. When she hadn't given her name, Jonathan commented that he just figured that Amanda and Avi had instigated the "no-name" nametag policy because of the previous facilitator's narcissistic behavior. Jake had figured it out when he found the interview with Dawn Fotopolus and had asked Amanda if the radio show host also had a local consulting firm.

One by one, they each shared how they had come to listen to the various interviews, which had obviously been hand-picked for each of them—but by whom and how? On that day that they had each listened to the shows, the integrated planning session had not even been scheduled. Wild.

Amanda and Avi smiled, as the previous week they had shared the exact same sentiment with one another about the show that they had each listened to. Both wondered how in the world that coincidence could have occurred. Now that they knew that the whole team each had the same experience, Amanda knew that it had to be the Grand Designer that had made it possible.

As the team was trying to work out the plausible explanations, Avi commented how odd it was that the host was a strategist that lived right here in Tampa. The other night when he was trying to get in touch with her, he saw the "813" area code on her website. Even though her company was local, her client base included multinational corporations and early stage businesses alike. In fact, she was even on the board of Rich Media Exchange, their first client to "trip-enable" the photos and videos on their portal site with their Toolkit. He didn't know how he missed the connection!

When Amanda had put two and two together, she found it even more bizarre that the local firm specialized in integrated planning, which was just what the doctor ordered for the Company, literally!

After she and Avi had talked about scheduling the planning session, she had checked out the facilitator's website and was very happy to see that she regularly worked with the investment community. In fact, she had advised some of the biggest names in the private equity field that invested in travel, and was an expert in the underlying technology used by most online travel tools, including theirs, and the global distribution systems that powered most travel sites. American Airlines had been the first one to launch their system commercially in travel agencies in the late '70s and she had written four books about global distribution.

Avi got goose bumps again and then slowly the fog began to lift. That was where he had met the Business Designer. She had been the CEO of Capture. He felt very foolish, but relieved that he had finally made the connection. He couldn't wait to get home and tell Sarah, since the three of them had worked closely together, albeit by phone. He knew her voice had sounded familiar, but once they figured out the radio show link, he thought that was the reason. Now he knew the rest of the story.

The team was tired and it was time to turn in. Whereas a few weeks ago he would have deferred to Amanda, Avi stepped comfortably back into his leadership role and deftly made that recommendation. Everyone gladly followed his lead and began clearing the table, getting their things together. As they headed out, they each stopped at the back table and grabbed their bag, with the notebook and pen inside. The team responsibly made sure that they were not leaving behind any beer and wine, winking at each other as they each took another one, happy for the bag to carry it to their room. Amanda quietly took two bottles of water, staying true to her promise to herself. Catherine opted for the sparkling water, in keeping with her training.

Everyone got into the elevator, but Avi had forgotten the book that Jake had given them. He told them to go on ahead. He would see them all for breakfast at 8:00 a.m.

As he walked back into the room, he stopped at the table that held the "no-name name tag" box and grabbed the small eraser and a pen. He felt strongly that he was supposed to erase "Proud Immigrant Entrepreneur" and replace it with "Game Changer." When he was done, he went back into the room and quickly found his copy of the book. It was only then that he saw the tagline: *A Small Business Survival Guide.*

He was looking forward to reading the book and to become better prepared for the upcoming IPO. And he was excited to see the outcome after tomorrow's session and even more jazzed to get the full, integrated plan from the Business

Designer and her team and dive in to implement the initiatives. He was shooting for 100% completion of the upcoming plan.

He looked at the book again and thought to himself how grateful he was that they were no longer small and he was sure after today that they were going way past survival. They weren't just going to change the game.

They were going to win.

Epilogue

The Mountaintop

"Success is not final, failure is not fatal,
it is the courage to continue that counts."
Winston Churchill

■ ■ New York | The Future | The Team ■ ■

Avi couldn't believe that it had only been a year and a half since the planning session. They had already accomplished nearly 100% of the integrated plan elements and they were just minutes from taking their company public on the NASDAQ Stock market in New York City.

As he entered the room, he saw the infamous Plexiglas podium with NASDAQ written in silver letters. But that wasn't what drew Avi's attention. And it wasn't the red box that housed the opening bell, which he would be ringing in a few moments.

No. Every fiber of Avi's being was tuned into the video playing on the multi-image screen behind the podium. He felt as if he were in a trance. Time stood still. After Catherine returned from her amazing climb of Mt. Kilimanjaro, her team, along with their marketing firm, had done an incredible job putting together the film that was being shown this morning.

It outlined the Company's history, including his own start in the travel industry at the Hilton in Tel Aviv, high up on the bluff overlooking the Mediterranean.

It then took the viewer to Avi's start in the tech industry, at MIT and DEC, to the Company's inception and

Photo credit: Hilton Hotels

the Firm's investment in 2016 to now, January 25, 2018, the day of their initial public offering.

Catherine smiled at the significance of the date. Another new beginning.

Not surprisingly, they used the mountain climbing metaphor, including a sunset picture Catherine had taken on her trek.

Photo credit: Joan O'Sullivan Wright

Avi was overwhelmed with emotion. Today he was at the summit, the Initial Public Offering (IPO) of his company. But this time, the sun was not setting, it was rising. *This is my company*, he thought. *No, it is our company. We made this happen.* Avi felt a deep, now comfortable feeling of pure joy.

■ ■ ■ ■

After the integrated planning session, the Company had shifted from the status quo to changing the game in everything that they did. The culture of the

Company was now one of intellectual curiosity and innovation, and one of joy! They had set up their office to support the new culture.

They had learned from Rich Sheridan, the author of *Joy, Inc.* that joy can be a competitive advantage and they learned that cubicles kill. They kill morale, communication, productivity, creativity, teamwork, camaraderie, energy, spirit and results. Their new office environment was more like a bunch of cozy living rooms. They learned from the best practices of other companies and even other industries to improve everything that they did and every product that they sold.

Avi had set up a library in the foyer of the office, making available a wide range of books to the employees, as well as to vendors, customers and prospects. They were organized by leadership, innovation, entrepreneurialism, growth and giving back. The library was Jake's idea, which made Avi laugh.

Of course, *The Improvisation Edge; The Go-Giver; Defy Gravity; Think Like Zuck; I'd Rather Be In Charge; Dare, Dream, Do; Zombie Loyalists; Accounting for the Numberphobic; Disrupt Yourself; The Freaks Shall Inherit the Earth; UP: Pursuing Significance in Leadership and Life;* and *Joy, Inc.;* were all on the shelf.

Each month, the whole team independently read a different book and discussed it in staff meetings. The staff was encouraged to recommend books to Jake for the monthly reading list and for the library. Jake loved this new facet of his job. He had even suggested creating the Game Changer Network in cooperation with the Facilitator.

Amanda had added one just last week that in the haste to prepare for today the team had yet to read, *The Grand Weaver*, by Ravi Zacharias. She hoped it would help them get to know the Grand Designer personally and perhaps even see how He had guided them all to listen to just the right radio show, as if it had been handpicked.

Catherine's friend, Sierra, had come in and done multiple workshops with the team to help them better understand how to communicate with one another and how to best motivate other members of the team. She even had Avi talking in the four-letter MBTI lingo when he talked about his team! He was definitely an ENTJ! Sierra also had him eating healthier, as each time she would come for a workshop, she would bring her yummy gluten-free snacks, which of course delighted Tim. She had recently started a blog of her great recipes for those who wanted to be healthier and had even gotten Jonathan on board!

Avi happened to know that Sierra had introduced Jonathan to one of her friends and he was a changed man, no longer best friends with the barkeep at the pub. On Friday nights, he could be found at the local high school football game (American football that is), watching his girlfriend's son play defense for the varsity team coached by Sierra's husband. In fact, he wouldn't be surprised if the old man broke down and turned in his bachelor card soon.

Catherine's husband, Andy, was the top performer on the sales team at the financial services company, and had recently been selected to set up a new practice that works with early stage companies seeking innovative capital solutions to fuel their growth. Andy had become close friends with Jake, who was teaching him all about the intricacies of Wall Street and different funding options. Amanda had noticed a new spark in Catherine and Andy's relationship, which she suspected was from her encouraging Catherine not to work late at night when he was in town.

Amanda's nemesis at the Firm had been brought up on sexual harassment charges and had been let go. Each time she walked past his old office, a slight smile would cross her face. After his termination, she had told the other partners about the disastrous offsite training, and the entire Firm now used the Facilitator for their portfolio company offsite sessions.

Avi and Amanda had interviewed many potential board candidates. They had decided on a young woman who had recently left her position as president of the company she had founded. Her firm had taken in outside investment, so she knew exactly where Avi was coming from. She had developed game changing technology for the attractions industry. Cecilia worked with the Business Designer and had also been mentoring Catherine, from a slightly different angle than Amanda. She was also good friends with Christine and Flo.

Cecilia was a natural in her new role, bringing entrepreneurial energy, as well as sales leadership experience. She was going to be here today to share in their triumph, but Avi hadn't seen her yet. His wife Sarah was excited, as they had worked together but hadn't seen each other in some time.

True to her word, Amanda enrolled Catherine in the Executive MBA program at the University of Tampa, and through her friend Maureen, even arranged for her to submit her assignments remotely as she did her Kilimanjaro trek in October. On the day that she started the program, Maureen had met her for tea at the end of the day at her favorite restaurant and had presented Catherine with an autographed copy of her book, *My Decade with Diana, the Perpetual Power of the People's Princess.* Catherine remembered thinking, *life just doesn't get any better than this.*

Amanda promised her an increase in pay that was "fairy-tale-ish" on completion of her degree and Avi gave her some aggressive job related milestones to reach over the two-year period, aligned with her course of study that would have bonuses attached to achievement of each one. Then, in a surprise move, Amanda also told Catherine that she and Stephen, who were back together, had decided to sponsor both Veronica and Connor with a full scholarship to the college of their choice. Amanda didn't want Catherine to be distracted by the financial challenges and the lack of savings. Catherine was completely floored at her generosity and didn't know how to begin to thank Amanda for all that she had done. On top of the Executive MBA, she now felt like she was on the CBS show *Undercover Boss*, although Amanda had been anything but undercover with her.

Since they were so close, Catherine couldn't resist asking her about what had happened with Stephen, as it was clear that he had come back home. They were acting like newlyweds when they were together, which was nothing short of a miracle. Amanda simply told her that when she was listening to the Crosby, Stills and Nash song that first day of the onsite, she wasn't thinking about business, but about her marriage. Stephen had already agreed to go to counseling with her and she knew that she had nothing to lose. But it was the song lyrics "change my life, make it right, be my lady" that reminded her that she was the one who needed to meet Stephen halfway. Like listening to the customer as a company, she had to listen to what Stephen needed in their marriage. The result was a harmony in their marriage that she had only dreamed of before. They had celebrated getting back together by going to the Crosby, Stills and Nash concert tour, which took place onboard the transatlantic crossing of Cunard's Queen Mary 2 in October. It was a magical way to celebrate their 25th anniversary.

In March, Amanda and Stephen were traveling back to Europe. This time it was to Warsaw spend spring break with Elise. Their son Ben was coming too and trying to figure out how to pack his fishing pole, as he heard that the pike there grew to as much as fifty pounds! She found it funny that Catherine's son and her son both were so passionate about fishing, especially since the girls were so close.

Tim and Catherine worked together on getting a Spanish version of their product out for Hispanics residing in the US. Their competitors had all launched products in Spain or in Latin America, but somehow had missed the largest Hispanic market of all, their own country.

When he heard that the restaurant was being torn down to build million dollar condos, Tim had hired Hernan from the Chart House to head up customer service for their Spanish-speaking clients. It had been amazing to watch him blossom in that role. Tim was an amazing mentor to Hernan.

And just yesterday, Tim had told Avi that Liz was pregnant, with twins! When Catherine heard, she reminded Tim that she was a twin. She still loved the unique closeness that she shared with her brother.

Every person in the company was now focused on the customer rather than on the profitability of their products and services. Their new customer-centric CIO, Sydney, had made a huge impact on development. Each new feature was seen through their customer's eyes and customer engagement was increasing exponentially. Her millennial view had impacted their mobile product and had opened their eyes to a whole new market for the product, international college students.

The Company and the new Game Changer Network had been featured on Bloomberg and Fox Business networks on Worldwide Business with Kathy Ireland, which had given them international acclaim. Kathy had loved not only their focus on innovation, but the fact that giving back and being customer centric were baked into the company DNA.

The Company had formalized its innovation fund, setting aside 10% of every dollar earned to support major, new initiatives. Catherine had already identified several new women owned entrepreneurs to look at for potential partnerships this year and together she and Amanda were already mentoring the CEOs. They might even use some of their innovation fund to invest in one or more of those enterprises.

They were all very clear on their direction and were using the Multiplica process for identifying customer needs and product value for each of their targets. Their customer conversions had gone through the roof on every one of their products.

The Firm was very happy with that development, since transactional revenue was the bread and butter of the Company. The team learned that structure didn't have to have a bad rap and that they needed to develop a long-term view, with days serving the weeks and weeks serving the larger, year over year goals.

Jake still worked with each one to understand the costs and the return on investment, but the exercise was empowering instead of debilitating. It was about getting to yes instead of finding a reason to say no.

The new focus impacted how they supported one another, as those teams that provided services for the front line realized that those employees were their customers too. Even the Executive team had realized that the employees were their customers. All of this significantly impacted conversion and retention rates, which were key performance indicators. And not surprisingly, employee satisfaction had increased significantly, reducing attrition.

Everyone loved the gigantic, backlit "dashboard" that was on the wall where everyone could see it. There were regular celebrations of success as they continually upped the bar on their performance, both in unit sales and profitability.

Avi knew that this excitement wasn't isolated to just him and the leadership team. Everyone seemed to be happier in their jobs. The Company was providing a great place for employees to grow careers and an excellent work environment to develop skills.

The customer intimacy orientation had immediately produced a higher level of profitability and growth than they had ever experienced. It was measurable and for the last three quarters, they broke every growth record, based on year over year performance. The Firm had escalated the schedule of the IPO to take advantage of the momentum that they had built. It was gratifying to see this acknowledgement of the team's efforts.

Each of the teams had embraced a new kind of collaboration with everyone working toward a unified outcome. From the leadership team on down, they had learned that the level and amount of trust you feel affects not only individual performance, but also the performance and profitability of the entire organization.

The various teams had learned to use building blocks, where the word yes was important, as well as allowing each person to build on the previous individual's ideas, reducing the chance that an idea was discarded because of a past negative attitude or some other bias. This process was so much more productive than traditional brainstorming. Additionally, they all practiced improvisation, fueled by regular visits to the improv club in Ybor City, thanks to Catherine!

The best thing was that with each new product and service release, they all owned the success because they used the improvisation techniques. The innate skills, philosophy, and behaviors of improvisation are radically collaborative and the team found that when they learned the skills needed to adapt and collaborate on such a high level, it intrinsically engendered trust.

Now they had a new form of equity—team equity. The results had been amazing and two new product ideas and travel widgets now provided the Company with a new revenue stream and complete marketplace differentiation. If they did fail in any way, they all knew how to go from "Oops to Eureka," a premise they had all learned from reading *The Improvisation Edge*, a book that Catherine had added to the library.

The Go-Giver was now required reading for new members of the sales and service teams. As a matter of both policy and principal, the sales team was now giving more value to customers than they took in payment. In fact, the whole team embraced all *Five Laws of Stratospheric Success* outlined in the book. After the integrated planning session, Jonathan had asked that *The Go-Giver* poster be hung prominently in the sales department to remind everyone of their goals. He even had laminated business size cards printed for each one of them to carry with them in their wallets.

It was clear that this was more than just a program or a slogan, as the team had in fact experienced "stratospheric" sales success over the last twenty months since the second offsite, another reason for the acceleration of the IPO.

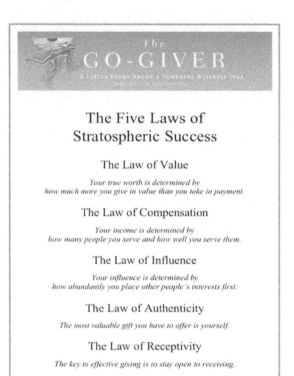

© Copyright Bob Burg and John David Mann

The entire team defied gravity in everything that they did. It started with the Customer Service and Operations teams, which had renamed themselves simply "Customer Care." They had gone through all of their processes and all of the policies and they retooled everything that got in the way of saying yes to their customers. Rebel Brown had called that, "Releasing the sources of gravity," in her book, "*Defy Gravity.*"

Next, they had found the value that would drive real growth for the Company—getting repeat business and referrals. This allowed the group to make a material impact on the Company. They no longer relied just on the sales team to bring in revenues. This was their fuel. It helped them locate the opportunities that were ready and waiting for the value that the Company had to offer them, thereby saving time and giving their customers new revenue opportunities.

Now, they were regularly practicing all the principles the executive team had first learned in the radio broadcasts that seemed to be hand selected for them. Avi still hadn't figured that one out, but after the significant investment of time that he had spent with Amanda, he now instinctively knew that he would just have to have faith. He had seen her put an autographed copy of *The Grand Weaver,* by Ravi Zacharias, on the shelf a few days ago at the office and he suspected it was just for him.

■ ■ ■ ■

Sarah broke his reverie. She had just arrived with the Business Designer. They had renewed their friendship from the DEC days and both of them had wanted to be there to support Avi and the team. Cecilia had arrived and she gave him a quick hug and warmly greeted Sarah and the Business Designer. Amanda and Jake both greeted him with a warm handshake, followed with a hug. One by one, Avi shook the hands of the other partners of the Firm. All of them were there. It felt surreal.

Amanda then introduced him to her husband, Stephen. They were holding hands and looked like they were on their honeymoon, even though he knew they had just celebrated their 25th wedding anniversary. He and Stephen were the same age and he suspected that they would become good friends. Amanda then introduced Avi to Maureen, her friend of Diana dress fame. He knew that she had been instrumental in assisting Catherine with getting into the Executive MBA program at UT. Catherine had shared her entire story with him and had even donated to their library the book Maureen had given her, *My Decade with Diana: The Perpetual Power of the People's Princess.* He shook Maureen's hand and smiled a warm smile filled with admiration.

Moments later, Bob Greifeld, the CEO of NASDAQ, was greeting him and his administrative assistant was reminding Avi that once Bob had given his opening remarks, Avi would come to the front, along with the whole team. They had rehearsed all of this yesterday, so he hoped he wouldn't get tongue-tied with his own remarks.

Amanda had surprised him yesterday by telling him that Charlotte Beers, of Ogilvy and Mather fame, had agreed to write his speech and that she would be there today to support them. Charlotte had been coaching Amanda since shortly after the planning session. Amanda had also spent some time with Tim's wife, focusing on nutrition and amping up her physical activity, as well as only treating herself to a glass of wine with dinner on weekends. As a result, she was down thirty pounds. The Business Designer had treated Amanda on her last trip to Tampa by taking her shopping with Wendi, her stylist, and now Amanda had a new look that suited her perfectly, yet still fit in well in her New York world.

Avi glanced over at Tim and Jonathan, who were talking to Catherine. She had her back to him, but just as he waved to them, she turned and smiled. He couldn't be happier than he was today, knowing that each of them had played an instrumental role in getting them here. It wasn't just a matter of them doing their jobs. It was the complete end-to-end shift in focus of the entire team over the last twenty months.

He knew it was almost time to get started. He turned to start moving toward the front and to his left was a group that he had to stop and greet. Peter, Chris, Olivier, Flo, Caryn, Christine, Roxy, John, and Jody had all been instrumental in getting them here. He gave each one of them a warm handshake and they each shared words of congratulations.

Just before he went up to the front, Catherine asked him to come over to the left of the podium where a long line of people stood. It looked like a receiving line at a wedding. Other than Mary Jo and Nicolas from their team, he didn't recognize any of them. He gave Mary Jo a quick hug, thanking her for all that she had done, gave Nico a strong handshake and a smile, then he turned back to Catherine before continuing.

At first, he didn't understand why she would take the time now to do the introductions, but as he shook each one's hands in succession, her timing became clear. He flashed back to the photomontage on the wall as you enter their offices, entitled, *The Influencers: Our Executive Village*.

"Avi, this is Karen Hough, the author of *The Improvisation Edge*. May I introduce Bob Burg and John David Mann? They are the co-authors of *The Go-Giver*. And this is Rebel Brown. She wrote *Defy Gravity*. I'd like to introduce Whitney Johnson. She wrote both *Dare, Dream, Do* and *Disrupt Yourself,* and is a very good friend of Amanda. This is Charlotte Beers, the author of *I'd Rather Be In Charge.* Charlotte stopped him from moving on for a second and said that she was happy that Amanda had understood the real title of the book. She smiled warmly and he moved on to meet Ekaterina Walter, the author of *Think Like Zuck.* He couldn't even speak when he realized that standing next to Ekaterina was Mark Zuckerberg himself. He humbly encouraged Avi to enjoy the day. "I remember not long ago ringing the bell myself. Mine was outside in the park with everyone posting selfies and videos to Facebook. Just remember Avi, you did it! Just enjoy."

After he caught his breath, Catherine continued walking him down the line. "Next is Tom Fishburne, the irreverent, *Marketoonist.*" Tom grinned as he shook Avi's hand, taking pride in Catherine's introduction. "Next is Chris Brogan." Avi said, "Ah, my favorite freak!" as he firmly shook Brogan's hand.

"Avi, I am pleased to introduce my new friend and fellow climber, Joan O'Sullivan Wright. As you know, she was my coach for my climb. She is also the author of a book titled, *UP: Pursuing Significance in Leadership and Life.* Avi reached out and gave her a hug. He also thanked her for introducing them to Senai Global, the non-profit organization that they had adopted as their philanthropic partner for 2017. He told her that he had enjoyed meeting Drew Harding, SG's founder, who had helped the company choose a high-impact project in Africa to back as a Company, helping to transform African people from victims of circumstance to victors of hope and change. Joan smiled and thanked him for his support.

"Next is Rich Sheridan. He is single handedly responsible for the new look and feel of our offices!"

Avi grabbed Rich's hand and pulled him into a bear hug and thanked him. He also said, "I didn't even realize that I was searching for joy in my life!" Rich smiled a knowing smile.

Then Catherine moved down the line said, "May I introduce Peter Shankman, Jake's new best friend and the author of *Zombie Loyalists.*" Avi laughed and shook Peter's hand firmly.

"Next is Dawn Fotopulos, the author of *Accounting for the Numberphobic.* Without her, none of us could have made it through the road trip!"

After shaking Dawn's hand, he smiled and turned back to look at everyone. For once in his life, Avi was speechless. He had to be the luckiest man alive.

All he could do was hold his hands out in silent gratitude to those standing before him. Before he turned to the front, he held his hands to his heart and smiled. His team and board members had now joined the authors, the members of the Firm, his wife, and the Business Designer.

As Bob Greifeld walked past him to the podium to start the program, he finally was able to say to the group words that seemed completely inadequate in their simplicity. He looked at each one and one by one he said "Thank you."

Bob was just starting his remarks, "I want to congratulate Avi and his team for their perseverance on the roadshow and raising $470 million over the last two weeks to fund their global expansion. This followed a record-breaking launch of their proof of concept of a new trip planning product in North America. In just twenty short months, they have totally changed the name of the game for the travel industry, or as Avi says, they have successfully turned the travel industry on its head. They have done this by putting the customer first and finally letting us plan our trips the way it should be done—to the actual places we are going and events that we are attending. After decades of being forced to do most of the work before we even began to plan our trips, we can now use the Company's tools to start with where we need to be. Bravo to the team for executing against this simple, but profound vision."

Bob then spent a few minutes talking about NASDAQ and how it has attracted many companies that have redefined the economy in the U.S. and that have promised to do the same thing around the world.

"Avi, please join me with your team for this important ceremony." Everyone clapped and Bob reached out to Avi to come to the podium with his leadership team. "While we are waiting for them, I'd like to read a short note from a dear friend of Avi's that couldn't be here today." On the screen was a smiling picture of Benjamin Netanyahu. Bob, proceeded to read a note from his dear friend Bibi, telling Avi how very proud of him that he was, mentioning their days together in primary school as well as at MIT. Bob finished by saying that it wasn't often that they had a message from a Prime Minister at an IPO! Avi was so choked up, he hoped that he would be able to give his speech.

His team walked around the life-size model of their stock ticker molded in their signature teal blue and walked past the podium and stood to his left. Avi got to the microphone and thanked Bob. He then told the audience, "I want to thank my team and the Firm, without whom I would not be here today. Our team is a rather unusual one and I want them all by my side to celebrate this important day in our Company's history. These people are a significant part of our story and I need to invite them to join me on my right."

He turned and invited the entire receiving line and the Business Designer to come to the front to stand at his side. They filed single file and joined together in front of the life-sized ticker symbol.

"You see before you, more than an executive team of a company about to go public and the design and development company and the private equity firm that got them there. You also see the executive village that stands behind them and beside them, propelling them toward their destiny. You will be surprised to know that some of them I am meeting face to face for the first time today.

"We have an irreverent cartoonist, who tells the truth about business through humor. He makes us laugh at ourselves and deal with the mischief that keeps us from success. Next to him is a social media legend who runs an amazing online group that selflessly provides insight and encouragement to entrepreneurs. And we have the entrepreneur of all entrepreneurs and yes, it is okay to take a photo and post it to Facebook! And, next to him is a group of authors and a radio show host that shared their time and messages unselfishly over the airwaves via the Internet, without compensation, not knowing who was listening."

Avi smiled a broad smile and looked from the group of authors to his team and back. "Well, I can tell you who listened—my team and I. I won't go into how and when, as I do have a bell to ring here, but suffice it to say, they have collectively shaped our beliefs, thoughts, words, actions, habits, and values. They have brought us here today. We each learned from their messages and their wisdom and we came together as a team to apply them. We are now living out our destiny and over the last last year and a half, I have also reached a personal goal of mine as a result."

Then, he decided to share something personal with the audience. He had clued in Catherine, so he saw her step out of the group and move over behind the ticker symbol. "As a company, we donate 10% of our revenues to the charity of choice of our clients. I am proud to tell you that today we are writing a check to Senai Global in the amount of $1 million dollars based on our fourth quarter revenues from our own self-service Toolkit."

With that, Catherine brought out an oversized check made out to SG and handed it to Joan. Avi hadn't known that Joan would be there, but he had asked Drew Harding, the founder of SG, to join them, so he now asked Drew to come up and join Joan to accept the check.

Avi continued, "We are not only a profitable company about to ring the NASDAQ opening bell, but we are also leaving a legacy to change lives for generations to come. There is nothing that could make me more proud today. What we found out over the last year and a half is that declaring your goals and your purpose makes them official and commits you to whatever it takes to get there. The most important component of our balance sheet is something that doesn't appear in print. It is measured in wells built in villages, families brought out of poverty, children having access to medical and dental treatment and good nutrition and young people rescued from human slavery."

"Just twenty months ago, with the help of a team of consultants from Tampa, we had our moment of declaration." He looked over to the Business Designer with a smile that she knew was just for her. "One of our team climbed Mt. Kilimanjaro this past year. Her coach, who is here today, told her that 'declaration of your purpose introduces the elements of risk, courage and responsibility. Once it's out of the box, it's impossible to put back in.' While she thought she was just coaching someone who would climb the tallest freestanding peak in the world, she was coaching all of us."

Avi paused for a moment smiling at the team before continuing, "I know now that you don't make it to the top yourself. Like it or not, twenty months ago we all stepped into the 'commitment zone.' Any goal we pursue, any climb we make that is worthwhile, will involve risk, commitment and investment. While Catherine was the only one to get to the actual physical summit of Kilimanjaro, our entire team this year reached our own personal summit—the IPO on the NASDAQ. Bob, thank you again for everything and thank you to those that have invested in us. This experience is incomparable." Avi wrapped up by saying. "Thank you to my entire extended team. It does indeed take more than the seed of innovation to build a company. Let me now share with you our company history."

With that, the amazing Company IPO video began to play, beginning with the sunrise image on Kilimanjaro from Catherine's trek.

The video went on, telling with music and pictures not only Avi's own history, including his Jewish roots, but how everyone on the team had come together to build this amazing company, effectively climbing their own summit. It also told the story of the customers across a broad range of industries that had helped them

© Copyright Joan O'Sullivan Wright, Mountain Musings Journal 2012

succeed in their proof of concept. Their logos were familiar to all in the room and Avi and Catherine shared a knowing smile as a major CRM company's logo was displayed in the video.

Seeing Joan at the IPO celebration reminded Avi of reading her *Mountain Musings,* when Catherine returned from her climb. Two things that had stuck with him. First, was the notion that there is no place for personal ego, pride or fear in the success of a team. Second, was the power of storytelling, and how our fellow team members get to know us through the telling of our stories. By knowing those stories, we can be the best for one another through the trek we call life. Joan said that, "shared stories circumvent judgment and banish internal fears." Both truths had been borne out by his team over the last year and a half in both their personal lives and in the business.

As the video continued to tell the story, Avi also found himself thinking about the scripture that Catherine had shared with him after her summit experience. Actually, it may have come from Joan's journal as well. It was Psalm 121, penned by his namesake David. If he remembered correctly, it said,

"I lift up my eyes to the mountains where does my help come from. My help comes from the Lord, the Maker of heaven and earth. He will not let your foot slip—He who watches over you and will not slumber."

Avi knew that through it all, the seemingly endless sleepless nights and bootstrapped days, his foot was absolutely steady. He was wise enough to know who gave him the courage to press on. As Joan had said in her climbing journal, it was "pure lunacy to think any of us could have done this by ourselves."

As the music swelled and the picture of the sunset from Kilimanjaro was displayed signaling the end of the video, Avi poised his hand to ring the bell, savoring the moment. It was 9:30 a.m. ET and he had to admit that this was it.

In the background, the perfect harmony of Crosby, Stills and Nash played softly.

Pure joy.

About the Author

"You who holds the stars and calls them each by name,
will surely keep your promise to me."
Take Courage, Kristene DiMarco

 **Chicke Fitzgerald** spent the first half of her career working for industry leading travel distribution technology and telecom companies, including American Airlines Sabre, Worldspan (now known as Travelport) and SITA Telecommunications. If you have ever booked travel online, chances are she has worked for or with the companies that made it possible.

She was frequently chosen for skunk works projects, including the leading-edge expense management system at AMR known as Capture, where she worked under the leadership of industry titan, Max Hopper.

Following her successful corporate career, she formed Solutionz in 1996 and has a proven track record as a game-changing technologist, creating innovative multi-channel solutions and business models for clients, as well as for her own companies.

Over the past decade, Chicke founded LeisureLogix, Solutionz Media and her latest venture, Solutionz Technologies, investing over $1.2 million of her own funds and raising $6 million in investment capital.

In 2007, she pioneered a new technology that shifts the travel booking process from city centers and airports to the place or event where people are traveling. In the second quarter of 2015 the Company launched the next generation of that platform, designed to take companies from simply having a Contact Us page to having an intelligent Visit Us page. In 2016 the Company added a graphical version of the widget as well as t-vite™, with embedded social network sharing and in early 2017 launched a self-service platform. Think AddThis™ for Travel. The premise behind the product is multi-dimensional:

Proximity Matters | Time Matters | Simplicity Matters | Choice Matters

Chicke commissioned Tom Fishburne, the Marketoonist™, to do a custom cartoon for the launch of the TripPlanz™ plug and play product to the events industry, focusing on the issue of saving time for meeting and event planners.

A highly sought after strategic advisor to the travel, media and financial services industries, including Wall Street and private equity companies, Chicke also hosts a weekly radio show, focused on innovation and growth strategies. The show and her Executive Village blog is also syndicated out over Travel Daily Media, a publication reaching over 50,000 travel industry professionals.

She is also an investor in Rich Media Exchange, a company with exciting integrated media technology for the travel and media industries.

Chicke welcomes strategic partners and investors who share her passion, particularly in the travel and events industries and location based services.

Chicke's faith and courage is core to her identity, as is giving back and mentoring others to discover their radical sense of purpose. Whether in her own ventures or those of her clients, her business focus is growth; 360-degree growth in both corporate and entrepreneurial environments.

Growth is achieved by ditching the status quo and by listening to the front lines who know the customer—customers are the keepers of the secrets of business success.

The Rest Of The Story
(aka acknowledgements)

It is often said that we all have a book inside of us, just waiting to get out. What you may not know is that writing a book begins long before the first word appears on a page. I'm not talking about laying out the story line or developing character profiles.

I began writing *the Game Changer* the day that I asked my parents if I could drop out of college in 1976. It was 32 years later that I walked into the bookstore at Atlanta Hartsfield Airport on a cold day in January and picked up a copy of *The Go-Giver.* I began reading it right away and finished as we pulled up to the jet bridge in Tampa. I was completely enthralled with the genre of the business fable.

It was March 2015 before the first words made it on the page. Through the process I learned so much about writing, about life and about me. I have so many people to thank for their support.

Thanks to those that read and commented on the early manuscripts, with a special thanks to MK Marsden and Suzanne Callaway for your honest feedback. You shaped the final product.

Thank you to Michael Fitzgerald, for 27 [mostly!] glorious years and for your unconditional love and support, through thick and thin. It wouldn't have been any fun without you by my side. Thanks for letting me work at all hours of the day and night so that this book and my current tech company could become a reality. And thanks to for bringing home the bacon these last few years, so I could pursue my dream and at the same time get to be a part of our kids' lives in a new way.

Thanks to my kids, Kiera and Sergey, for your unconditional love and the inspiration for a number of the characters of *the Game Changer*. Kiera, we are so proud of you and your independence and courage in selecting the University of Warsaw for your Masters' degree in Psychology. And Sergey, we don't know what you will end up pursuing, but we know that your love for fishing and sports and your amazing personality and smile will take you far. And Fidelia, without you, I could never have had many of the successes that my current company are built upon. Thanks for being "big sister" and role model.

And to JoJo who kept me company on the late nights at the keyboard, walking across it when you were hungry, I am sorry that there was no cameo role for you in the book, but since cats can't read, I suspect you'll never know. I love you.

Many of my dear friends and colleagues made it into cameo roles in *the Game Changer*. Chris, Flo, Helene, Roxy, Cecilia and Shannon you are my inspiration and the Board of Directors of my life. Tony, you saved Michael and I more than once since we met in 2000. I am so grateful for your belief in me in being Employee #1.

An equal number are not mentioned in the book, but nevertheless played a part in making me who I am. Kathleen and Buff, you were always there for me as both friends and sisters and you both made our January 25th's much easier. And our parents, who are no longer with us, provided the foundation for believing that I could do and be anything that I wanted. They also showed us true unconditional love, which made choosing a life based on my faith so much easier. I couldn't have made it through the tough times without it. Faith has been to my journey, as breath is to life.

Thanks to my freshman English professor, Ruth Givens, who gave me an A on my paper, *The Value of Experience Versus Education*, the catalyst for me quitting school after one semester and fearlessly pursuing my career instead.

For every boss that I ever had, both good and bad, thank you for the role that you played in shaping me into a leader.

For Bob Wilhelm, thank you for promoting me to VP of Sales of Travelink, from my role in service and for you and Don pushing me out of my comfort zone. Now you know the rest of the story about me being sick those three days after my promotion.

For Terry Jones, who gave me so many cool projects, who taught me how to be creative and use technology to communicate and who showed me how to think big, thank you. To Al Ramacciotti, thanks for letting us buy your company. You were my first acquisition at age 29. To DEC and Sun and Unisys, thanks for taking a chance on a technology that was truly game changing. And for Bob Crandall, thanks for that day that you told me that it was my project that failed, not me. You didn't have to do that, but you did and it had far reaching impact.

To Don Russell, my first investor, thanks for believing in me and more importantly, for still being my friend after we lost the bet on our first technology company.

To those who played a role in my consulting firm and my various other ventures, thanks for believing in me and my vision. Annette Hogan, you have been my rock.

Thanks to every author that I have ever interviewed for enriching my life and for my producer, Pattie Brinkman, who made my radio show possible. Special thanks to one of my "author angels", Gail McWilliams, a very talented, but blind author, who just before her cancer diagnosis and her untimely death, introduced me to Bruce Barbour, my literary agent, who introduced me to David Hancock at Morgan James Publishing, I am eternally grateful for learning about vision and courage from a woman who spent the better part of her adult life blind. I will definitely "see you" on the other side! And more importantly, you will "see" me.

To the rest of the Morgan James family, thank you. A special word of gratitude to Margo, Jim and Nickcole, without whom, this book would never have seen that once elusive book store shelf!

To Kulin Strimbu, a very special thank you for letting me come along side you to help you on your entrepreneurial journey and to launch the Executive Village on Travel Daily USA and for trip enabling the photos and videos on the Rich Media Exchange platform. You are a game changer and have made me laugh more than any other person in my entire life, even during our dark and scary days when it would have been easier to give up. I believe that one day you will be the one behind the Plexiglas pedestal taking your company public—from my mouth to God's ears!

To Paolo and Mary Jo, you came into the project at a pivotal time for us. Thank you for believing.

For my Executive Village, in the Appendix I have a link to my video thanks for your individual contributions to *the Game Changer*. And thanks to both Tony and Magnus for the roles that you played getting the audio and video ready for the launch of the book. To the characters of my book, thank you for letting me live vicariously through you, as a younger version of myself having kids early, as the male version of myself as CEO, as the educated version of myself and by expressing my own hopes, dreams and fears as a part of the story. Art indeed imitates life.

There are many of you that have no idea that you contributed to this book. If you touched my life in any way, as friend, colleague, client, pastor, teacher, mentor, it is like a stone tossed into a pond. It is very likely that you had a ripple effect on my transformation from college dropout to game changing technologist and author and to the hundreds of thousands of people that I have been able to reach through my radio shows, blogs and my consulting work. I share my legacy with you.

To Erik Williams, Flo Lugli and Peter Giamalva and all who pre-ordered *the Game Changer* and contributed to making the project a success, I am humbled.

Thanks to all of you that have made it this far and who have allowed me to share my story in a way that can hopefully inspire you to change something about your game today.

But most of all I want to thank the "Grand Weaver" himself for leading me to that table in Concourse B in Atlanta and making The Go-Giver jump off the table into my hands. I was meant to read **that book, that day**.

Appendix

Our Executive Village

Throughout the story you have just read, there were many individuals that had an impact on Avi's team and as a result, on the Company as a whole, as well as on its investors, the Firm. We call them our Executive Village and here we highlight a few of them so that you can learn more about each one and how their message can help your organization grow and change the game in your industry.

Chicke's real life village includes cartoonists, artists, photographers, musicians, collectors and hundreds of authors and business people that have played a role in her life and her company. That network is extensive and it would take another book [or two or three] to introduce you to them.

Here, and on the Game Changer Network site, we provide you additional insights into their specific contributions and we showcase over 300 interviews that Chicke Fitzgerald has done over the past decade on her weekly radio show. Join us and you can procure your very own Village, tailored to your needs and to your challenges, listening to the shows on demand, commercial free.

EDITORS NOTE: This section includes QR Codes. You can obtain a QR Code reader in the app store for your smart phone and then easily read these symbols with your phone by holding the phone over the code.

Each QR Code is linked to a unique webpage, which provides a short video of the truths that the team gleaned from the interview with the author and how they fit into *the Game Changer* story. The author QR codes provide a link to the original radio interview. It provides a bio of the author and a link to order the book.

If you do not have a smart phone or a QR Code reader, you may simply visit the Game Changer Network site and click on The Village in the navigation.

The Game Changer Network

Access the QR Code to hear an introduction to
the Game Changer **by Chicke Fitzgerald**

The Game Changer radio show is hosted weekly by Chicke Fitzgerald, aka the Business Designer. She interviews authors and experts on topics of leadership, growth, entrepreneurialism, innovation and giving back. It is syndicated over BlogTalkRadio, iTunes and Travel Daily Media. The Game Changer Network provides several membership options to take advantage of the wide array of content on the site and to connect with other Game Changers on a regular basis.

Tom Fishburne—The Marketoonist

Access the QR Code for a video introduction to Tom Fishburne and his work.

Marketoonist is the thought bubble of Tom Fishburne, a career marketer and cartoonist. Chicke discovered these tongue-in-cheek cartoons and began using them in her consulting to playfully point out the "elephant in the room" to her clients. Tom is now designing custom cartoons for the new TripPlanz™ product launch and we hope that you enjoyed how we used his cartoons to punctuate *the Game Changer* story.

Karen Hough—The Improvisation Edge

Access the QR Code for a video introduction to
Karen Hough and the Improvisation Edge

Karen Hough is the Founder & CEO of ImprovEdge, and has been using improvisation as an engaging learning tool for over 12 years. Chicke read Karen's book in 2011 on an airplane and was fascinated with the potential for the use of improv techniques in business. Less than 24 hours after reading the book, before she even interviewed Karen, she tried one of the techniques mentioned in Chapter 2 of *the Game Changer* with wildly successful results.

Bob Burg and John David Mann—The Go-Giver

Access the QR Code for a video introduction to
Bob Burg, John David Mann and The Go Giver

Although for years Bob Burg was best known for his book *Endless Referrals*, over the past few years it's his business parable, *The Go-Giver*, coauthored with John David Mann, that has captured the imagination of his readers. John has a passion for great writing and appreciates the exquisite beauty of a powerful idea expressed in words. He was an advisor on the professional editing of this manuscript.

The Go-Giver played a pivotal part in the birth of *the Game Changer*. In 2009, after reading the Go-Giver on a flight from Atlanta to Tampa, Chicke knew that she wanted to write a business book using their allegorical style. She then contacted Bob and John to be guests on her radio show, then known as Solutionz Live! In the ensuing years, they have become friends and have worked together many times since that initial encounter.

Rebel Brown—Defy Gravity

**Access the QR Code for a video introduction
to Rebel Brown and Defy Gravity**

Rebel Brown has spent over 25 years in high technology consulting as a recognized market/product strategist and turnaround expert. Chicke first interviewed Rebel in 2010 and the two became fast friends. Rebel is a powerful speaker and guides leaders to shift away from yesterday's beliefs about their business and into fresh perspectives that fuel innovative go-to-market strategies. Once you hear Rebel's personal backstory, you will know that this is a woman that truly defies gravity in all that she does.

Joan O'Sullivan Wright—Up, Pursuing Significance

**Access the QR Code for a video introduction to
Joan O'Sullivan Wright and UP, Pursuing Significance**

When Chicke first encountered Joan, it was because she had read her statement about how climbing Kilimanjaro can change your life and was fascinated to learn more about her experience. A decade ago, Chicke had a mentor and business partner that had climbed both Kilimanjaro and Everest. She was the inspiration for Catherine's climb in *the Game Changer*.

From Joan's fictional mentoring in the story, Catherine learned the value of allies, and expert guidance, in the pursuit of significance in her own life. She also learned to appreciate the brilliant guidance provided by the leaders in her life, and how to tap the support that "climbers" provide to each other.

Charlotte Beers—I'd Rather Be In Charge

**Access the QR Code for a video introduction to
Charlotte Beers and I'd Rather Be In Charge**

Throughout her illustrious career, Charlotte Beers has been a CEO, a Chairman, and Undersecretary of State, and the first woman to appear on the cover of Fortune Magazine. Chicke interviewed Charlotte in 2014 and when she began writing *the Game Changer*, she knew that Charlotte's story had to be woven into the narrative. She was the perfect person to give direction to Amanda, who used her insights to encourage Avi. Charlotte Beers provides inspiration for women everywhere and her book gives a practical blueprint of elegant solutions for making this climb to being in charge and finding meaning and joy at work.

Ekaterina Walter—Think Like Zuck

Access the QR Code for a video introduction to Ekaterina Walter, Think Like Zuck and the Power of Visual Storytelling

Ekaterina Walter led strategic and marketing innovation for Fortune 500 brands such as Intel and Accenture. Branderati, the start-up she co-founded, was acquired by Sprinklr, where she now serves as Global Evangelist. Chicke first interviewed Ekaterina in 2013 and in 2017 will interview her on life after Intel and her latest book, The Power of Visual Storytelling. With her Russian heritage, there was an immediate connection, as Chicke's son was adopted from Vladivostok in 2003. In *the Game Changer*, with Avi's fictional story and his own Russian heritage, she was a natural foil for him to help him "think like Zuck."

Peter Shankman—Zombie Loyalists

Access the QR Code for a video introduction to Peter Shankman and Zombie Loyalists

Peter Shankman is an author, entrepreneur and corporate keynote speaker. He is a worldwide connector, recognized globally for radically new ways of thinking about customer service, social media, PR, marketing, advertising, and ADHD. Chicke first met Peter when he first founded HARO (Help a Reporter Out) and has interviewed him on multiple occasions. They share a passion for cats and for space.

Whitney Johnson—Dare, Dream Do and Disrupt Yourself

Access the QR Code for a video introduction to
Whitney Johnson and Dare, Dream, Do and Disrupt Yourself

Chicke first interviewed Whitney in 2012 to talk about Dare, Dream, Do and again in 2016 when Disrupt Yourself was published. They share a passion for innovation and empowering teams to do the right things and driving corporate innovation through personal disruption.

Whitney's background in the financial community coming up through the ranks as a real-life Working Girl, a la Melanie Griffith's character in the movie of the same name, made her a natural as the fictional dear friend of Amanda in *the Game Changer*.

Dawn Fotopulos—Accounting for the Numberphobic

**Access the QR Code for a video introduction to
Dawn Fotopulos and Accounting for the Numberphobic**

Dawn Fotopulos is an experienced entrepreneur and small-business turnaround expert. She has rescued hundreds of small businesses from financial disaster. Her book helps executives with companies of all sizes make sense of the finer points of accounting. She makes it interesting and even fun.

When Chicke interviewed Dawn in 2015, she had just started working on the book framework and it made total sense for Dawn to play a key role in *the Game Changer*. Thanks to Jake, the fictional CFO, she "helped" the executive team get comfortable with their numbers before the IPO.

Chris Brogan—The Freaks Shall Inherit the Earth

**Access the QR Code for a video introduction to
Chris Brogan and the Freaks Shall Inherit the Earth**

Chicke first began following Chris Brogan when she launched her radio show in 2009. She was trying to master social media as a new channel for distribution and Chris was an icon in social networking. When *The Freaks Shall Inherit the Earth* came out, Chicke knew that it was the perfect book for the Facilitator to be reading, as the sub-title *Entrepreneurship for Weirdos, Misfits, and World Dominators* was how the Facilitator often saw herself before she left the safety of corporate life.

Rich Sheridan—Joy, Inc.

Access the QR Code for a video introduction to Rich Sheridan and Joy, Inc.

One of the key themes of *the Game Changer* is joy. Finding joy in your work is an essential quotient in being successful individually and providing a culture of joy is to a company as clean air is to our ability to survive as a race.

Rich Sheridan has documented his quest for Joy in *Joy, Inc.* and when Chicke interviewed him, she knew that he had to play a role in *the Game Changer*, impacting not only the no-cubicle office environment of the Company, but also adding joy as a business goal to Avi and his team.

Ravi Zacharias—The Grand Weaver

**Access the QR Code for a video introduction to
Ravi Zacharias and the Grand Weaver.**

While Chicke has not interviewed **Ravi Zacharias** (yet), his book the Grand Weaver plays a subtle, yet powerful role in *the Game Changer*.

That book, published in 2007 by Zondervan, begins with a simple story of a man who seeks out the company that wove the beautiful saris worn by brides in India. What he finds in a small town in Northern India shows him the model of how the Grand Weaver guides us and makes sense of all of the different threads of our lives, making something beautiful not only out of the brilliant blues and reds in our experiences, but that the browns and the blacks of our lives also accentuate the resulting work of art. Zacharias is masterful in how he delivers God's message in such practical, relatable terms, visualizing the Father as the master weaver and the son, sitting at his feet, learning from and responding to His guidance.

In 1974 Chicke heard Corrie ten Boom, the author of The Hiding Place, speak in Milwaukee about her time in Ravensbruck prison camp near Berlin. Ms. ten Boom used a similar metaphor, although hers was about God as a weaver of the tapestry of our lives.

In the ensuing years, Chicke had often talked about the knots in her own life and the beauty of the resulting scene on the front of a tapestry once you could see it from God's perspective. So when she read about the loom and the colored threads and the saris in the Zacharias' work, the story immediately resonated with her and she loved the picture of God as the Grand Weaver.

In *the Game Changer*, Avi, the CEO of the Company, initially sees the capital raise as one of the dark elements in his life. Using ten Boom's metaphor, it would be one of the knots on the back of his own metaphorical tapestry. It is only when he sees that investment as one of the highlights, that he can turn around the tapestry and see not the jumble of knots and random threads, but instead could see the beautiful picture of what could and would emerge.

Avi's struggle is symbolic of Fitzgerald's own struggle with the concept of raising capital, but her deep faith in Zacharias' Grand Weaver gives her confidence that her own story will end up like the wedding sari, as a work of art.

The Others

Access the QR Code for a video introduction to the others that played a role in The Game Changer.

There were many others mentioned in *the Game Changer* that played a role in the telling of the Company's story. From Max Hopper and Bibi Netanyahu, to the authors of The Startup Nation, to the former owner of Princess Diana's dress collection, to a musician that Chicke has known since childhood, to two of the early believers in Chicke's current company—the people that make a company successful are often too many to mention.

The video about the "others" in *the Game Changer* provides color to why Chicke chose an Israeli man as the CEO of the fictional Company, when she could have (and many that know her have said that she should have) chosen a woman to play that role. It also provides insight as to why she chose Bibi as his best friend and protector in childhood and throughout his early days as an entrepreneur. Chicke also shares why positioning his heritage (read gender, race, educational background, etc.) as a strength versus a liability was the right thing to do and how that relates back to you and your business endeavors.

■ ■ ■ ■

It is our hope that understanding the backstories behind all of the players in *the Game Changer* will open up new avenues to you to change the game in your own life and your own company, whether small or large, or whether you are in fact "in between successes".

We want to hear from you. Please join the Game Changer Network and become an extended part of our village.

www.thegamechanger.network

Morgan James
Speakers Group

www.TheMorganJamesSpeakersGroup.com

We connect Morgan James published
authors with live and online events
and audiences whom will benefit
from their expertise.

9 781683 504962